International Winter Festivals

Projects and Patterns for Holiday Gifts, Greetings, Ornaments, Decorations and Classroom Displays

Written and illustrated by
Marilynn G. Barr

Cover by Marilynn G. Barr

Copyright © 1993, Good Apple

Good Apple
1204 Buchanan St., Box 299
Carthage, IL 62321-0299

SIMON & SCHUSTER *A Paramount Communications Company*

Copyright © 1993, Good Apple

ISBN No. 0-86653-712-0

Printing No. 9876543

**Good Apple
1204 Buchanan St., Box 299
Carthage, IL 62321-0299**

This book is dedicated to
B-Dot,
the Bean
and all the children I have known

GA1429

Table of Contents

GA1429

Table of Contents

GA1429

Introduction

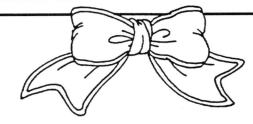

International Winter Festivals is a collection of patterns and activities based on the origins of customs and traditions practiced during the winter holiday seasons in countries around the world.

Although the celebration of Christmas is a Christian tradition, it has become recognized by many as a time of joy, hope, peace on earth, and goodwill toward all people. Traditions and customs vary between countries and religious beliefs. Some have changed over time yet still retain symbolic origins and many have remained the same for centuries. Many foreign customs were carried to new territories around the world by settlers and as a result the celebration of Christmas became many customs and traditions rolled into one.

Today it's a season when we can share joy, hope for peace on earth, and goodwill towards all the people of the world.

International Winter Festivals features interesting facts on the origins of traditions and customs, hands-on cut-and-paste activities for gifts, greetings, decorations, ornaments, bulletin board displays, songs, games, and holiday cooking ideas. Activities include materials lists, diagrams and directions, and illustrations of completed projects. Each section is easily identified with repeating borders. Blank border pages are included for writing activities and to use as frames for student artwork. Large, easy-to-cut-out patterns are also included for younger students as bulletin board displays or for take-home gifts. The open design of ornament patterns encourages individual creativity and is ideal for use as name tags.

May the spirit of the many holiday seasons of winter be with you and yours.

GA1429

AFRICA

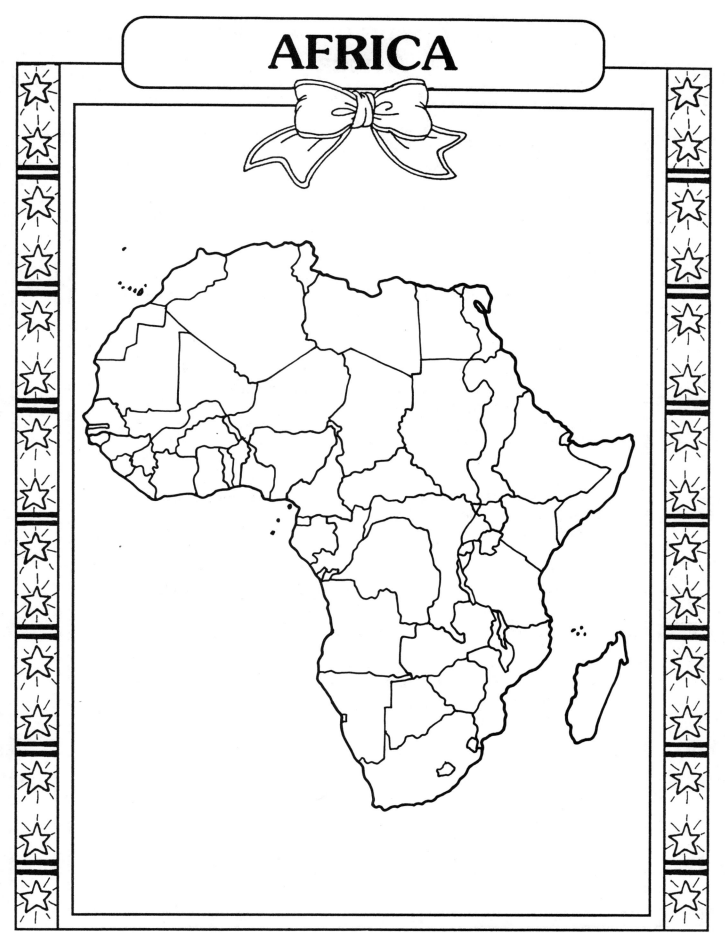

The Congo

Religious ceremonies fill this holiday season in the Congo of Africa. Families and friends in each village gather to share meals in celebration of the spirit of joy, hope, and brotherhood.

South Africa

South Africans celebrate Christmas in December. The summer climate brings families to the beaches and the mountains where they celebrate with games, singing, dancing, parading the streets with bands, and open-air lunches of traditional turkey or roast beef, mince pies, pork, yellow rice with raisins, vegetables, and plum pudding.

Ethiopia

Ethiopia's Christmas is observed on January 7, recognized as Three Kings' Day when the Christ Child was visited by three kings bearing gifts to honor his birth.

Ghana

In Ghana the celebration of Christmas is similar to the American and British. However, instead of coming through a chimney or from the North Pole, Father Christmas comes from the jungle.

Flowers and palm branches decorate homes. Children sing chants of the coming of the Christ Child and a giant evergreen or palm tree adorns their place of worship.

GA1429

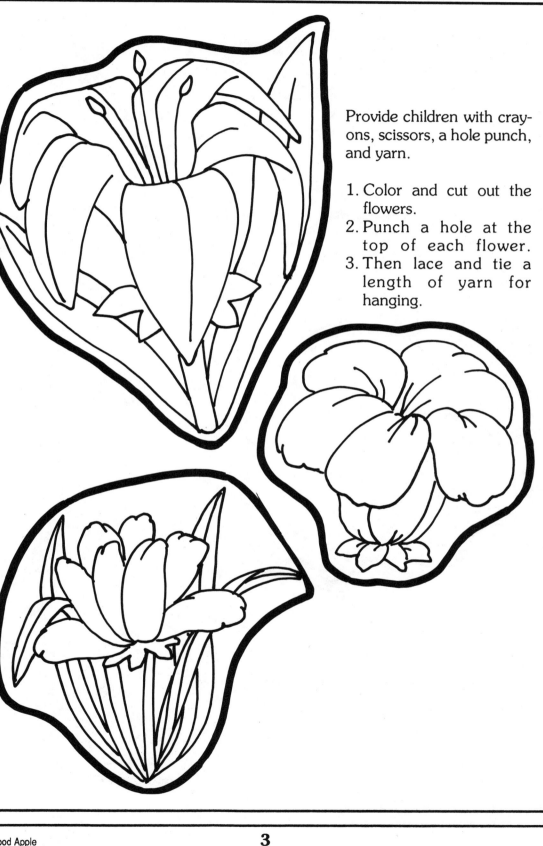

Provide children with crayons, scissors, a hole punch, and yarn.

1. Color and cut out the flowers.
2. Punch a hole at the top of each flower.
3. Then lace and tie a length of yarn for hanging.

Provide children with crayons, scissors, a hole punch, and yarn.

1. Color and cut out the flowers.
2. Punch a hole at the top of each flower.
3. Then lace and tie a length of yarn for hanging.

1. Color, cut out and fold the card along the dotted line.
2. Then write a holiday message inside.

Greeting Cards

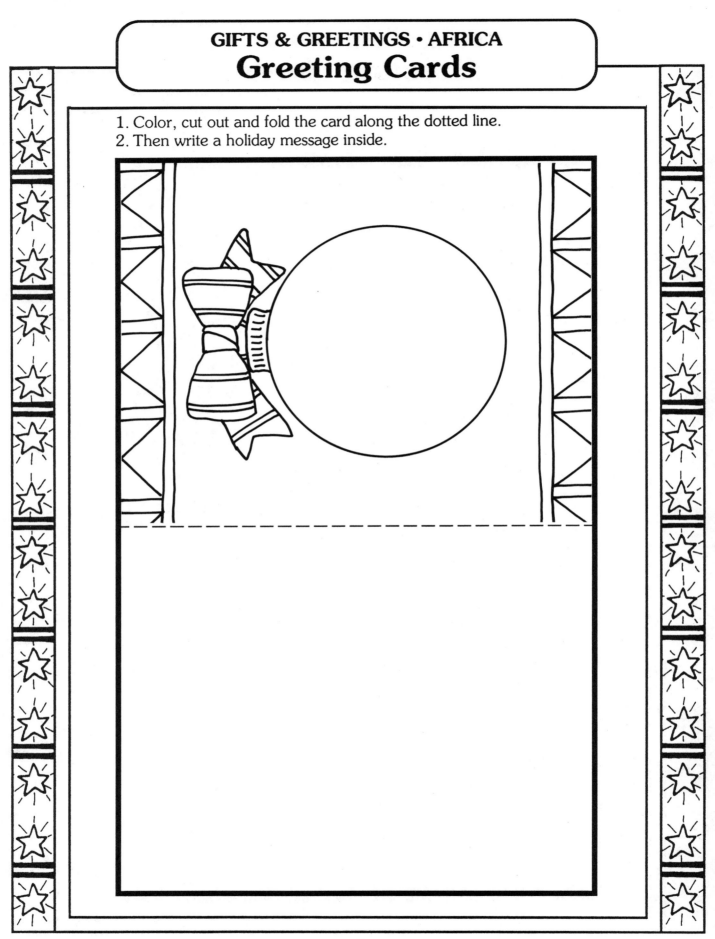

1. Color, cut out and fold the card along the dotted line.
2. Then write a holiday message inside.

Animal Tree Ornaments

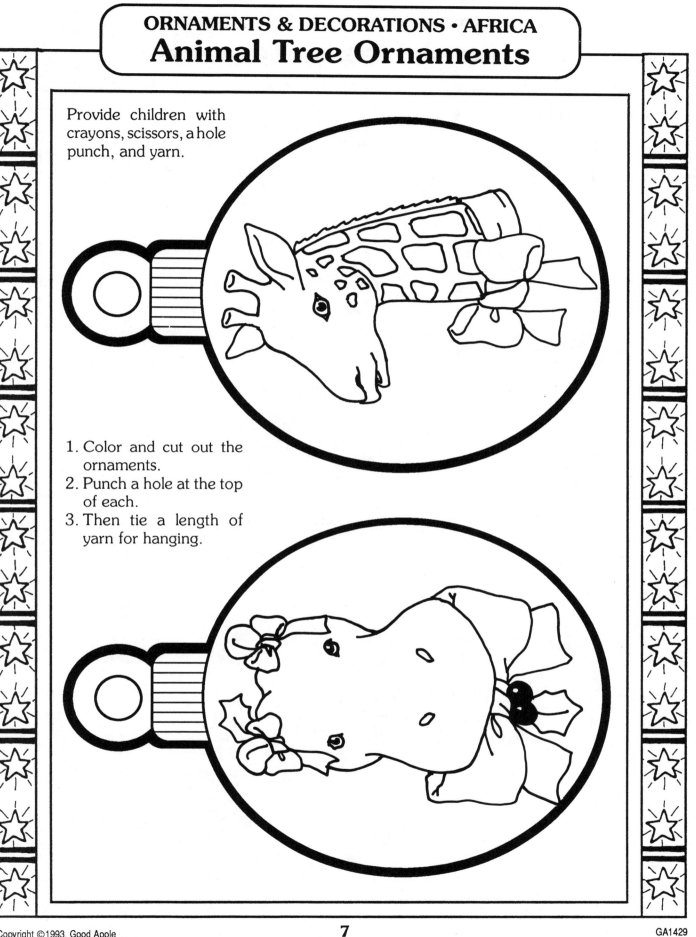

Provide children with crayons, scissors, a hole punch, and yarn.

1. Color and cut out the ornaments.
2. Punch a hole at the top of each.
3. Then tie a length of yarn for hanging.

GA1429

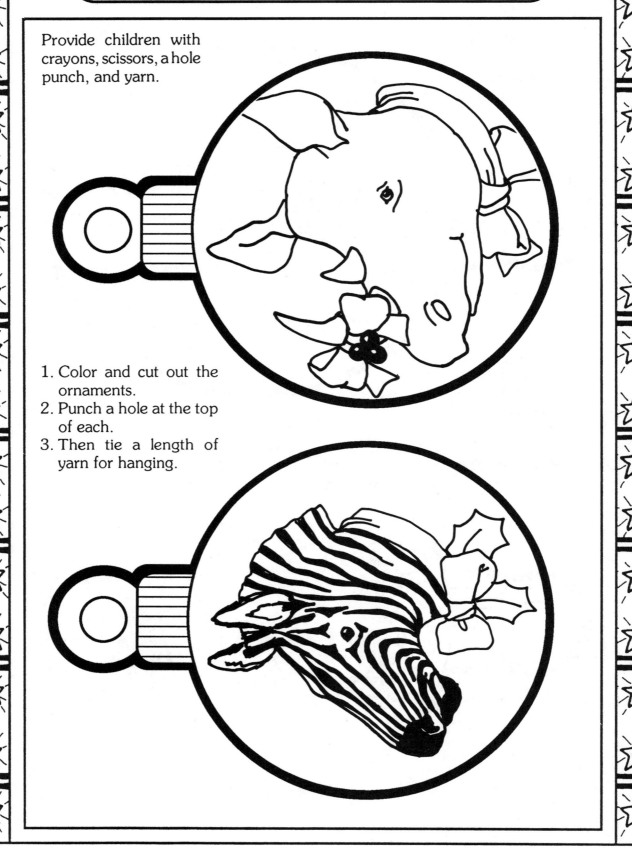

Provide children with crayons, scissors, a hole punch, and yarn.

1. Color and cut out the ornaments.
2. Punch a hole at the top of each.
3. Then tie a length of yarn for hanging.

Animal Tree Ornaments

Provide children with crayons, scissors, a hole punch, and yarn.

1. Color and cut out the ornaments.
2. Punch a hole at the top of each.
3. Then tie a length of yarn for hanging.

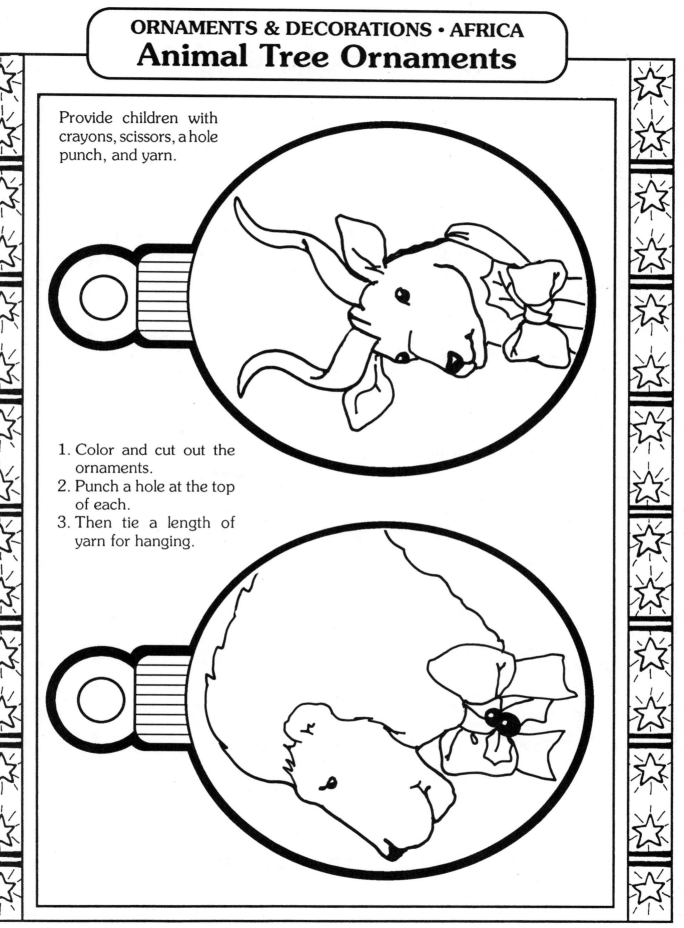

GA1429

Animal Tree Ornaments

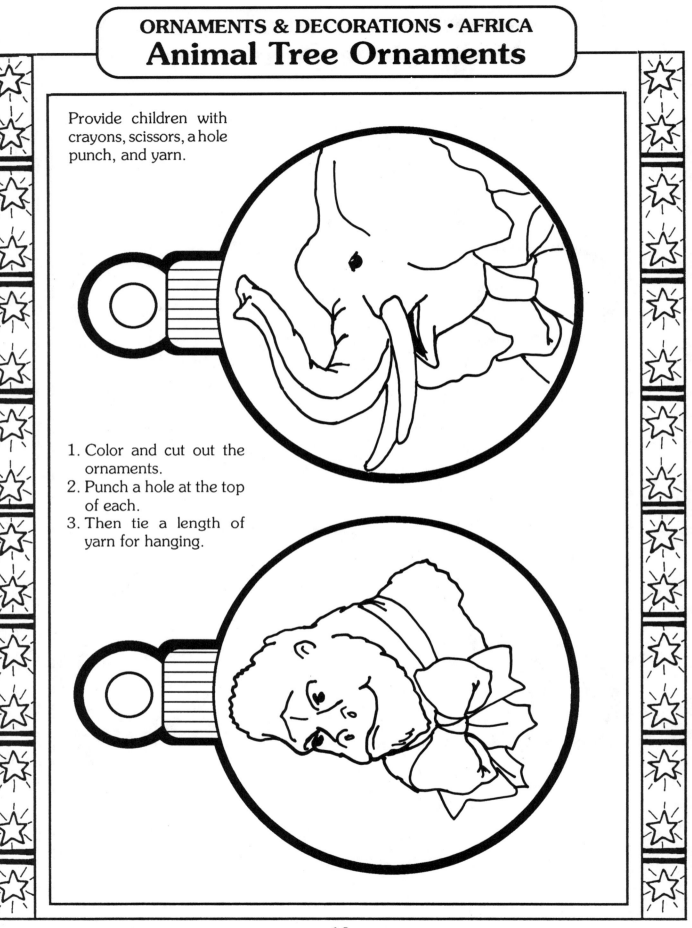

Provide children with crayons, scissors, a hole punch, and yarn.

1. Color and cut out the ornaments.
2. Punch a hole at the top of each.
3. Then tie a length of yarn for hanging.

Provide children with crayons, scissors, a hole punch, and yarn.

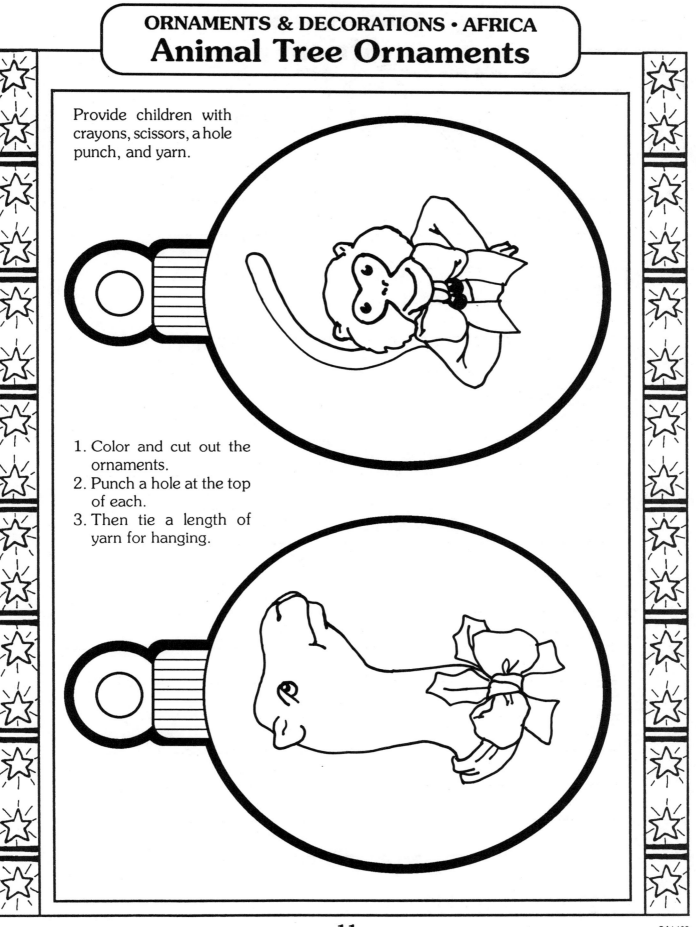

1. Color and cut out the ornaments.
2. Punch a hole at the top of each.
3. Then tie a length of yarn for hanging.

GA1429

CHRISTMAS IN
Africa

_____

_____

_____

_____

_____

_____

_____

_____

_____

_____

_____

_____

_____

_____

_____

_____

_____

_____

_____

_____

_____

ANTARCTICA

GA1429

Antarctica, the continent that surrounds the South Pole, is the coldest place on Earth. People cannot live on this continent because of the extreme temperatures and lack of plant life. However, many animals and birds that live near Antarctica's coastal waters are found on the covers of greeting cards, included in wrapping paper designs, and fashioned into holiday ornaments and decorations.

Your students will delight in making holiday ornaments and gifts with the patterns on pages 15-21. Reproduce the patterns for tree ornaments, greeting cards, or paper plate wreaths for lovely take-home gifts.

Tree Ornaments
Reproduce one or more patterns on pages 18-21 for each child. Provide children with construction paper circles, squares, and rectangles; yarn; scissors; glue; crayons or markers; and a hole punch.

Have children color and cut out the patterns and glue each one to a colored construction paper shape. Show how to glue a yarn border around the pattern. Punch a hole at the top and tie a length of yarn for hanging.

Greeting Cards
Oversized greeting cards always get lots of attention. Provide each child with his or her choice of an animal pattern, a 12" x 18" (30.48 x 45.72 cm) sheet of construction paper, crayons or markers, scissors, glue, and a variety of craft supplies to create Antarctic holiday greetings.

Paper Plate Animal Wreaths
Provide each student with green construction paper holly leaves and red berry circles, an animal pattern of his or her choice, a paper plate, crayons or markers, scissors, glue, yarn, a hole punch and yarn to fashion their own holiday animal wreaths for take-home gifts.

Provide students with appropriate supplies to make tree ornaments, greeting cards, or paper plate take-home gifts as listed on page 14.

Provide students with appropriate supplies to make tree ornaments, greeting cards, or paper plate take-home gifts as listed on page 14.

Provide students with appropriate supplies to make tree ornaments, greeting cards, or paper plate take-home gifts as listed on page 14.

Provide children with crayons, scissors, a hole punch, and yarn.

1. Color and cut out the ornaments.
2. Punch a hole at the top of each.
3. Then tie a length of yarn for hanging.

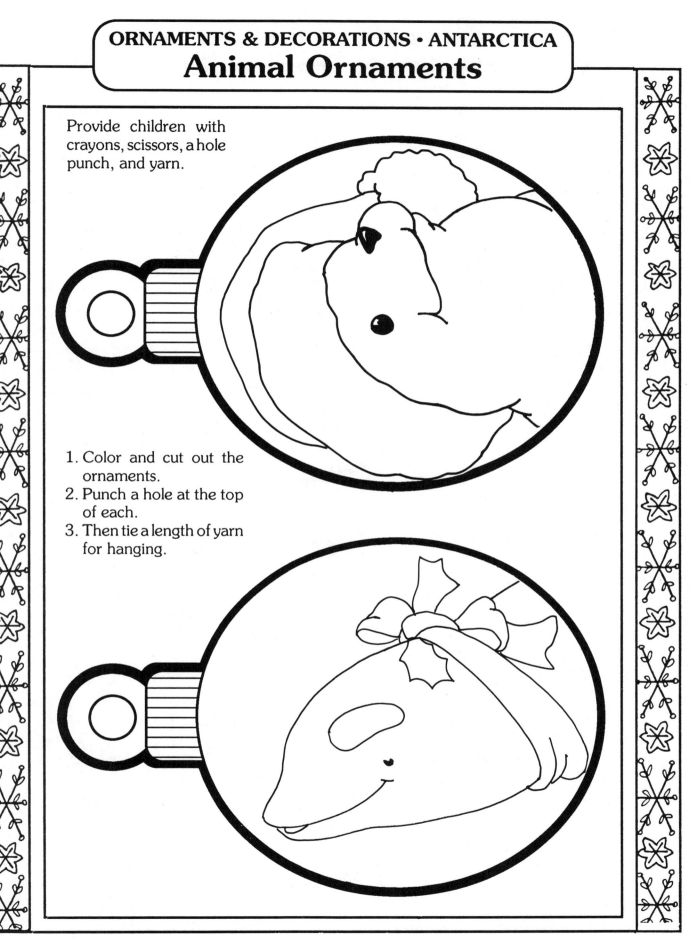

Provide children with crayons, scissors, a hole punch, and yarn.

1. Color and cut out the ornaments.
2. Punch a hole at the top of each.
3. Then tie a length of yarn for hanging.

GA1429

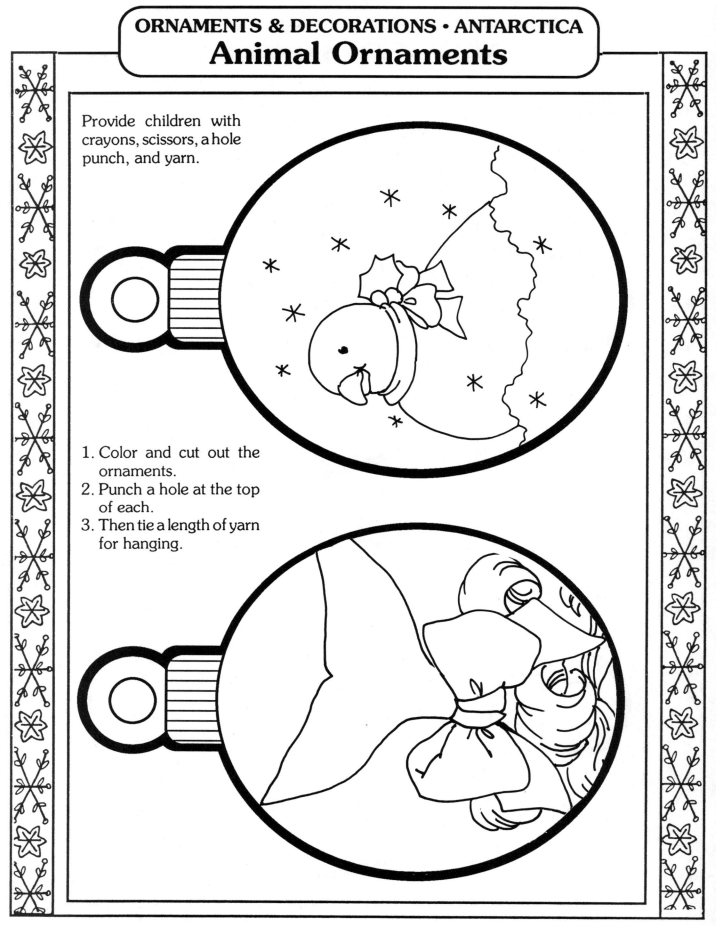

Provide children with crayons, scissors, a hole punch, and yarn.

1. Color and cut out the ornaments.
2. Punch a hole at the top of each.
3. Then tie a length of yarn for hanging.

GA1429

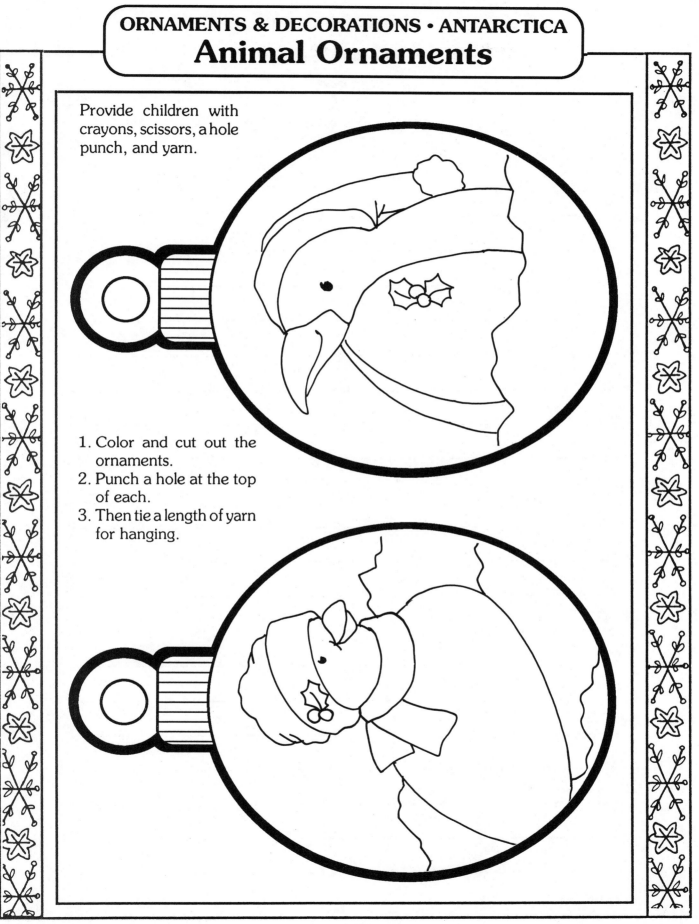

Provide children with crayons, scissors, a hole punch, and yarn.

1. Color and cut out the ornaments.
2. Punch a hole at the top of each.
3. Then tie a length of yarn for hanging.

GA1429

CHRISTMAS IN
Antarctica

ASIA

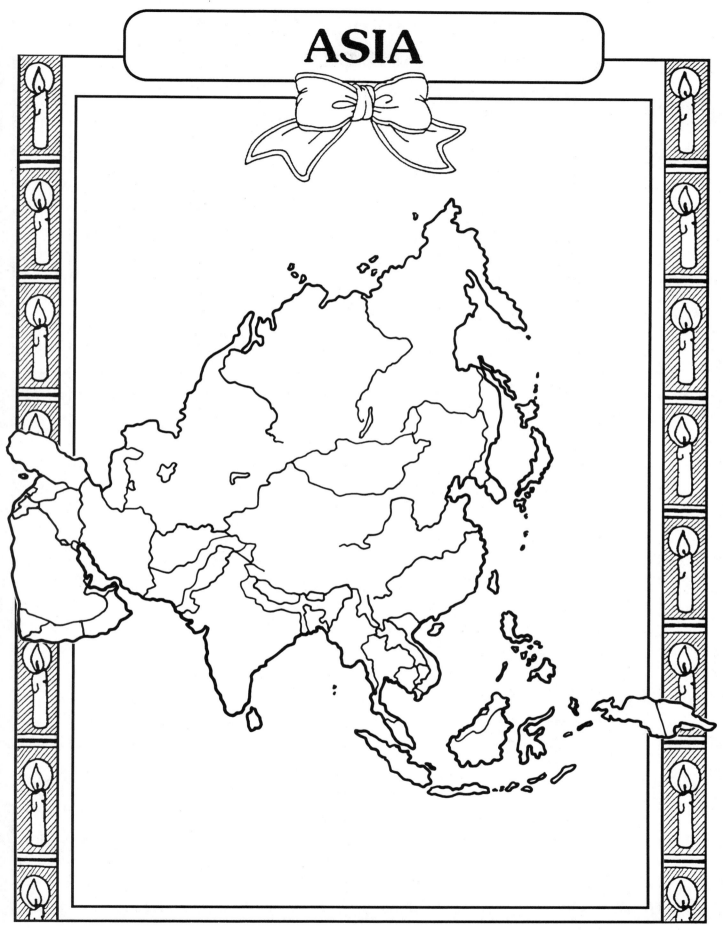

23

Armenia

Unlike the traditional Christmas with trees and Santa Claus, in Armenia lighted candles are set in the center of the table to commemorate this holiday.

Gifts are exchanged between children. Older friends traditionally stick coins into apples. Children enjoy keeping tabs on the one who collects the most apples stuffed with coins.

In another gift exchange, keeping with the spirit of the traditional Santa Claus, children climb to the roof of a house and lower a small basket down a neighbor's chimney to be filled with candy and homemade gifts.

Reproduce these patterns for each student. Provide each child with a sheet of green construction paper, a hole punch, crayons or markers, scissors, glue, a bright ribbon, and holiday treats.

1. Color and cut out the patterns.
2. Fold the apple and apply glue where indicated to form a pocket.
3. Glue the apple to a sheet of green construction paper and cut around the apple leaving a border of green showing.
4. Write a holiday message on the back.
5. Punch a hole and tie a ribbon to the stem of the apple.
6. Insert the coins in the pocket for a holiday gift, or substitute the coins with a holiday treat to hang on your tree.

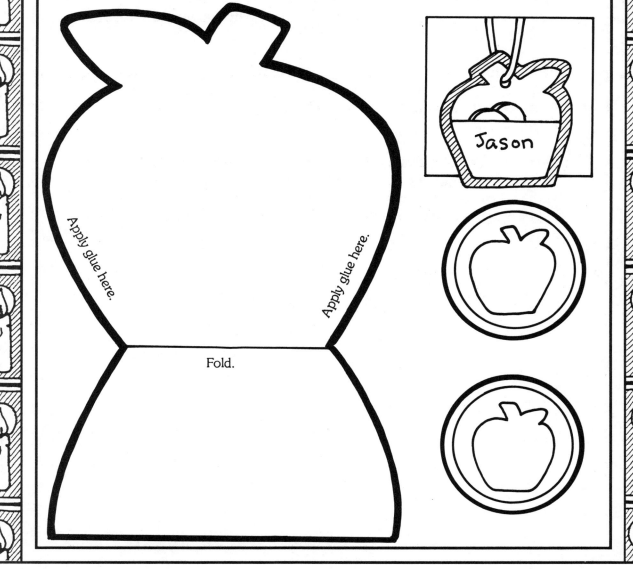

China

In China, Christians celebrate Christmas the same as other countries with traditional holiday shopping, cooking, and exchanging of gifts. Homes are decorated with paper chains, flowers, and lanterns. Santa is called *Dun Che Lao Ren* which means "Christmas Old Man," and children hang stockings to be filled with presents.

For the Chinese *Yuan Tan,* the celebration of Chinese New Year, which falls between late January and February, is equally as festive as Christmas. Each new year is represented by one of twelve animals. Decorations change to coincide with each new animal.

Families prepare for the new year festivities with a fresh coat of red paint on front doors, decorative red paper scrolls, candles, and flowers. And because each new year is considered each person's birthday, everyone receives a gift.

On the last day of the year the eldest male seals the luck in the house with strips of red paper. The family then begins their traditional celebration, ending the evening with a feast. And at midnight the children bow to the elders and the eldest male breaks the seal on the door to let in the new year.

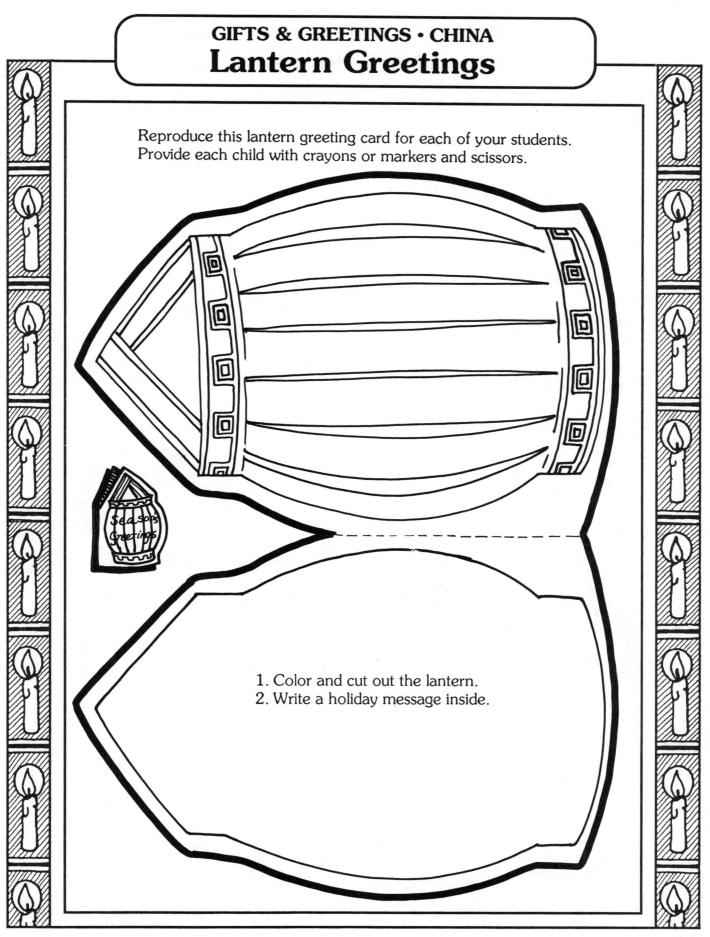

Reproduce this lantern greeting card for each of your students. Provide each child with crayons or markers and scissors.

Season's Greetings

1. Color and cut out the lantern.
2. Write a holiday message inside.

Red Packet

On New Year's Eve children receive "red packets" containing lucky coins and sometimes these red packets are found under pillows.

Provide your students with crayons or markers, yarn, and the patterns on pages 28-29 to make take-home "red packet" gifts.

1. Color and cut out the patterns.
2. Glue the medallions to the outside of the envelope.
3. Punch a hole in flaps B and C of the envelope.
4. Lace and tie a length of yarn through each hole.
5. Write a holiday greeting on the back of each coin and insert in your "red packet."
6. Fold flaps and tie a bow to close the envelope.
7. For variety, cut out pictures from magazines of favorite things and glue to construction paper coins to make personalized "red packet" gifts.

Medallions

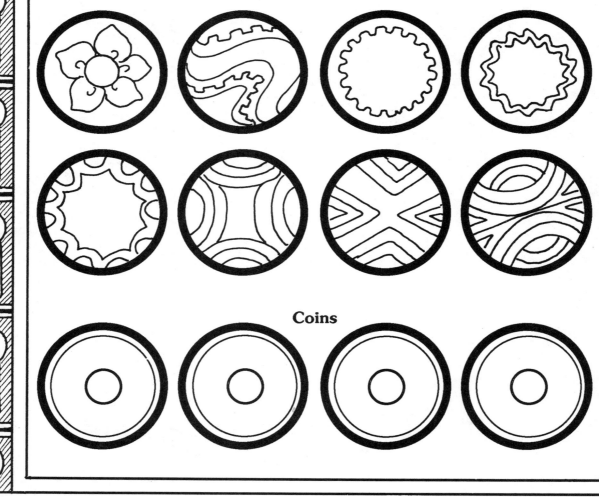

Coins

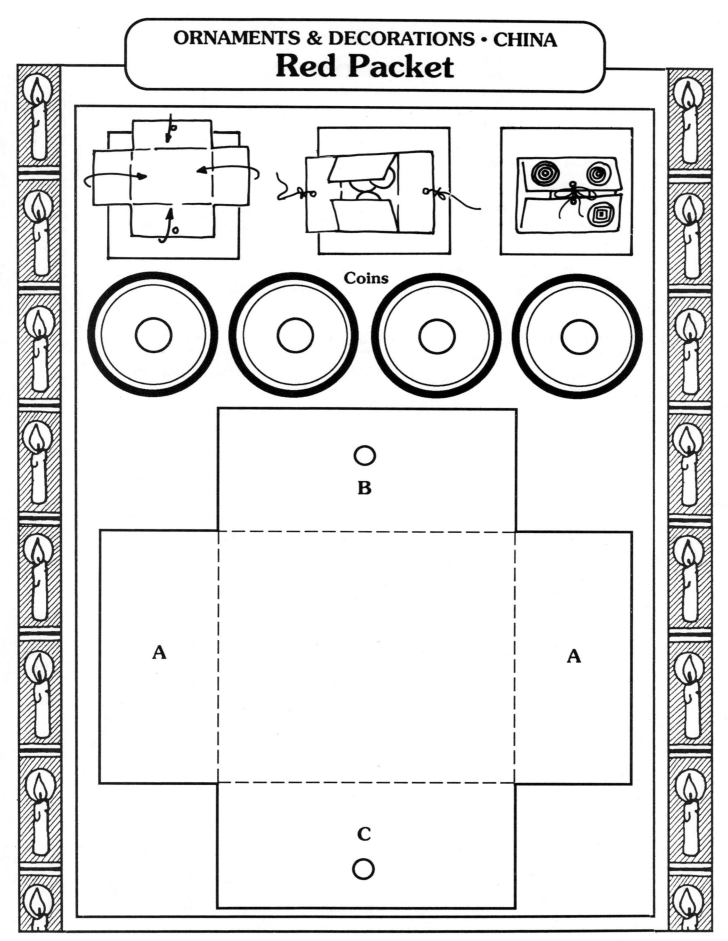

Coins

B

A

A

C

GA1429

Dim Sim Biscuits

The Chinese prepare a variety of tasty holiday foods like spring rolls, more commonly known as egg rolls, and dim sim, nut and sugar-filled red and white dumplings.

Divide your class into small groups and recruit parent volunteers to help with this class cooking activity. Although we are substituting homemade dumplings with canned biscuits, children will enjoy making these red and white dumplings symbolic of the Chinese dim sim.

Provide each child with crayons or markers, scissors, a toothpick, a lantern pattern, and a sheet of aluminum foil for a Chinese New Year snack.

Ingredients:

  4 cans of biscuits
  white icing
  red gel icing
  maple syrup and chopped
    nuts mixture (Prepare
    ahead: 1/2 cup [120 ml]
    syrup to 1 cup [240 ml]
    nuts)
  powdered sugar
  a toothpick

Yield: 32 biscuits

1. Open and separate canned biscuits (one biscuit per student).
2. Gently knead biscuit and flatten on aluminum foil.
3. Place a spoonful of nut mixture in center of biscuit, fold sides up and over to cover nuts and pinch closed.
4. Bake in oven per directions on package. Allow to cool.
5. Spread top with white icing and decorate biscuits with red gel icing and sprinkle with powdered sugar.
6. Color and cut out the lantern.
7. Tape a toothpick to the back of the lantern and insert in biscuit.

Provide your students with crayons or markers, scissors, glue, 3" (7.62 cm) colored construction paper circles, a hole punch, and yarn to make these twelve Chinese New Year ornaments.

1. Color and cut out the patterns.
2. Glue each animal on a construction paper circle.
3. Punch a hole at the top of each ornament.
4. Lace and tie a length of yarn for hanging.

Tree Lantern

Reproduce the lantern patterns on pages 32-33 on construction paper for each child. Provide crayons or markers, scissors, and glue to make holiday displays for the classroom or as take-home gifts.

2.

3.

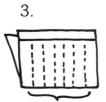

Cut on dotted lines.
Stop at dots.

4.

5.

1. Color and cut out Pattern A.
2. Apply glue to the tab, roll and secure it as shown.

Pattern A

Apply glue here.

GA1429

Tree Lantern

3. Draw a holiday scene on the blank side of Pattern B. Then fold it in half and cut along the dotted lines. Stop at the dots.
4. Apply glue to one end of Pattern B and attach it to the edge of the construction paper roll (Pattern A). Do the same at the bottom.
5. Then glue each end of the handle to the inside of the lantern as shown.

Pattern B

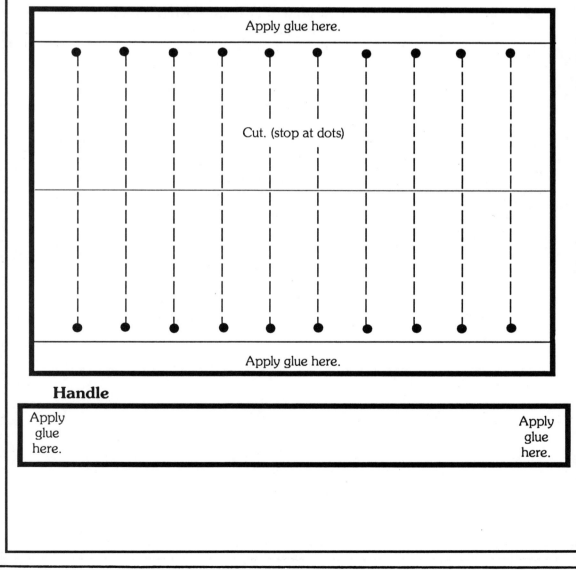

Apply glue here.

Cut. (stop at dots)

Apply glue here.

Handle

Apply glue here.

Apply glue here.

India

The night of lights, *Diwali* which means "row of lights," greets the holiday season in India.

Legend differs with each region. In some areas people say that Diwali celebrates the return of Rama and his bride, Sita, to the throne after being exiled for fourteen years. Others believe that it marks the destruction of Narakasura, who stole the jewels of Aditi, mother of the gods. And still others believe that Diwali dates back to when Lakshmi, the goddess of riches, was freed from captivity. Whatever the origins of Diwali, cleaning, whitewashing and decorating homes with dipa lamps, candles, holiday lights, garlands of bright colored flowers and painted designs of birds and flowers are welcome traditions.

After each household, dressed in their best clothes, shares a festive breakfast, families visit with friends and relatives and exchange gifts. Children buy firecrackers, painted clay and paper figurines and toys. The day ends with a visit to see dancing bears and performing monkeys. And then, with millions of lights lighting the night, families watch exploding fireworks in the sky.

Dipa lamps, tiny clay oil lamps are traditionally used to decorate homes for Diwali. Reproduce this dipa lamp pattern for your students to color, cut out, and assemble. Decorate your classroom bulletin board, door, desk tops, and windows for an Indian holiday celebration. Have children assemble dipa lamps on colored construction paper for take-home holiday gifts. Decorate a class tree with a dipa lamp garland by attaching student-made lamps to crepe paper streamers or ribbons.

Provide students with crayons or markers, scissors, glue and yarn.

1. Color and cut out the patterns.
2. Glue the clay lamp on the dish.
3. Glue the flame on the clay lamp as shown.
4. Glue yarn to the lamp as shown.

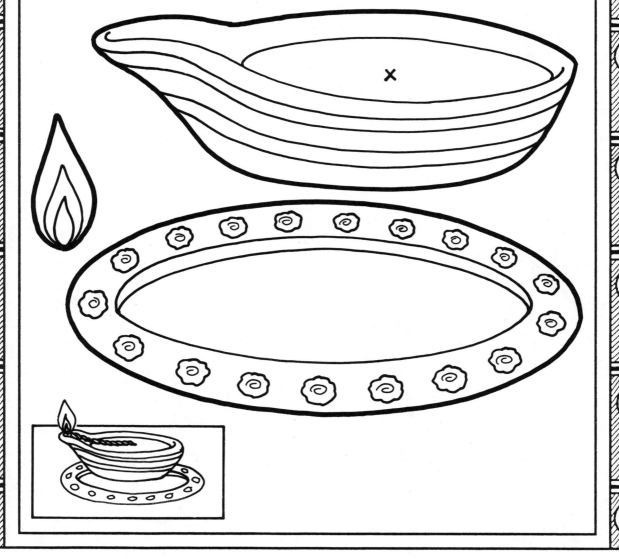

Use the patterns on pages 36-37 to decorate classroom walls, doors, and desks. Have children color, cut out and glue the patterns to black construction paper silhouettes, punch holes and attach yarn hangers.

1. Color and cut out the patterns.
2. Glue each pattern on black construction paper and cut around the pattern. Leave a black border around each pattern.
3. Punch a hole at the top of each bear and attach a yarn hanger.

GA1429

1. Color and cut out the patterns.
2. Glue each pattern on black construction paper and cut around the pattern. Leave a black border around each pattern.
3. Punch a hole at the top of each monkey and attach a yarn hanger.

GA1429

Reproduce these patterns for brightly colored flower garlands to decorate the classroom or for take-home gifts.

Provide students with crayons, scissors, glue, and a crepe paper streamer. (Note: For longer garlands, make multiple flower copies.)

1. Color and cut out the flowers.
2. Glue the flowers to a crepe paper streamer.

Use this pattern along with the diwali flower patterns on page 38 to create lovely place mats for take-home gifts.

Reproduce this pattern on yellow construction paper and provide students with flower patterns, crayons, scissors, glue, and an 11" x 17" (27.94 x 43.18 cm) sheet from a grocery bag.

1. Color and cut out the vase pattern.
2. Color and cut out the flower patterns.
3. Glue the vase and flowers on the grocery bag place mat.
4. Write a holiday message on the place mat.

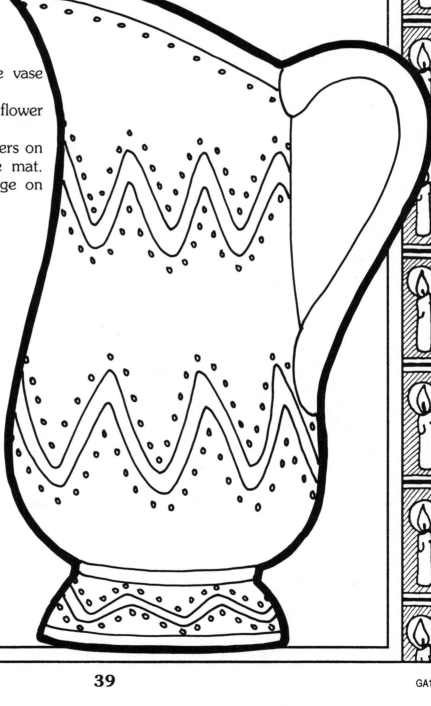

GA1429

Diwali Birds

Reproduce the patterns on pages 40-41 for children to make lovely, keepsake gifts to take home for the holidays. Provide children with crayons, scissors, glue, yarn, and a hole punch for a variety of gift ideas.

For a holiday decoration:
1. Color and cut out the bird, cage and bow patterns.
2. Assemble and glue the patterns on a colored sheet of construction paper for a lovely holiday poster.

3. Write a holiday message at the top of your poster.

For a holiday ornament:
1. Color and cut out the birds.
2. Glue the bow at the top of the triangle.
3. Punch a hole at the top, lace and tie a length of yarn to hang on your tree.

40

Diwali Birds

For a holiday greeting card:
1. Color and cut out the bird, cage and bow.
2. Arrange and glue the patterns on a folded sheet of construction paper for a greeting card.
3. Write a message inside the card.

41

GA1429

Turtle Paperweight

Ask parents to send clean, small margarine tubs (lids included) and newspapers to school for papier-mâché paperweight gifts.

Reproduce the feet, tail and eyes on green construction paper, and provide students with paint, scissors, glue and a variety of craft supplies to complete this project.

1. Fill the margarine tub with sand and glue the lid in place.
2. Have children layer strips of newspaper dipped in adhesive—one part white glue, one-half part water to make the turtle's body.
3. Demonstrate how to make and attach the turtle's head by wrapping newspaper strips around a crumpled piece of paper.
4. When the glue has dried, paint and decorate your turtle.
5. Cut out and glue on the feet, tail and eyes.

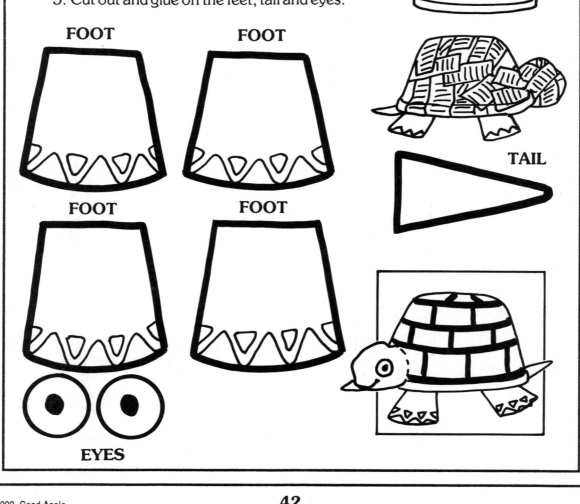

FOOT   **FOOT**

FOOT   **FOOT**

TAIL

EYES

GA1429

Iran and Iraq

Iran

In Iran, the land where the wise men, *Magi,* came from, Christmas is called *The Little Feast.* And it's believed that the trees bow their heads on the eve of Three Kings' Day, usually January 6th, to honor the birth of Christ.

Iranians begin their holiday celebrations on December 1, when people refrain from eating meat, eggs, milk or cheese. Then the Little Feast begins after religious services on December 25. Although gift giving isn't practiced, children receive new clothes to wear for the celebration.

Iraq

Christians in Iraq commemorate the holiday season by reading of the birth of the Christ Child. Bonfires in courtyards is a traditional custom. When the bonfires die out, everyone jumps over the ashes three times and makes a wish.

On Christmas day after religious services, the religious official touches a member of the congregation with his hand and that person touches the one next to him and so on until everyone has received the "touch of peace."

GA1429

Tree Ornaments

Provide your students with craft tissue paper, a large brush, glue, and brown construction paper tree trunks for lovely tree ornaments or displays for your class bulletin board.

1. Color and cut out the tree pattern.
2. Tear small scraps of colored tissue paper.
3. Brush a layer of glue over the treetop pattern.
4. Place scraps of tissue paper on the tree, layering different colors as you go.
5. Continue brushing layers of glue and attaching tissue paper scraps until the treetop is covered.
6. Now apply glue to the edge of the branches on the tree trunk and attach your treetop.

GA1429

Reproduce the patterns below for each student. Decorate your class bulletin board with this symbol of peace and brotherhood; then allow your students to take home their Wreaths of Peace to decorate their homes.

Provide each child with crayons or markers, a hole punch, a paper plate, paint, scissors, glue, ribbon, construction paper, and yarn.

1. Trace and cut out your hand on a sheet of construction paper.
2. Paint the paper plate your favorite color.
3. Punch a hole at the top of each hand pattern.
4. Lace and tie a ribbon through the holes.
5. Glue the hands on the paper plate as shown.
6. Punch a hole at the top of the plate.
7. Lace and tie a length of ribbon to the top of your Wreath of Peace to hang.

Christians who live in Israel celebrate Christmas in much the same manner as Christians in other countries. Another joyous holiday is also celebrated during the winter months in Israel by non-Christians, Hanukkah.

Hanukkah is the eight-day celebration of the triumph of the Jewish people over Gentile overlords who were keeping them from expressing their Jewish faith twenty-one centuries ago.

When the Maccabees reclaimed the Holy Temple in Jerusalem, they had only enough lamp oil for one day to light the great menorah (candelabrum). To their surprise, the candle burned for eight days, and for two thousand years the Jewish people have celebrated this special event.

Today, Jewish families still celebrate Hanukkah by lighting a nine-candle menorah over the period of eight days. The candle in the center of the menorah, the lighter candle or *shammash,* is used only to light the other eight candles. On the first night one of the parents lights the shammash; then the candle on the farthest right is lit, and each evening another candle is lit to symbolize a new day. When the lighting ceremony is over, families join in games and young children receive small gifts.

One traditional gift is a *dreidel.* The dreidel is a four-sided spinning top with the Hebrew characters for *nun, gimel, hay,* and *shin* on each side. Today these characters have different meanings than that of the original twenty-one century old event—*nikhts* (nothing), *gantz* (everything), *halb* (half), and *shtell-arein* (put in), terms used in a game played by both young and old. Each player has an equal number of tokens and in turn he or she spins the dreidel. When it stops, the player receives or loses tokens and the winner is the one who holds all the tokens.

GA1429

Hanukkah Menorah

Provide your students with wallpaper scraps, colored construction paper, yellow tissue paper or scraps of aluminum foil for flames, crayons, scissors, glue, and the patterns on pages 47-48 for festive Hanukkah menorahs to display on your classroom bulletin board or windows.

1. Color and cut out the menorah.
2. Color and cut out the candle patterns.
3. On the first day glue the shammash in the center and one other candle on the right side of the menorah.
4. Glue a tissue paper flame to the shammash then to the candle on the right.
5. At the end of each of seven days, glue a candle and flame to the menorah.

Shammash

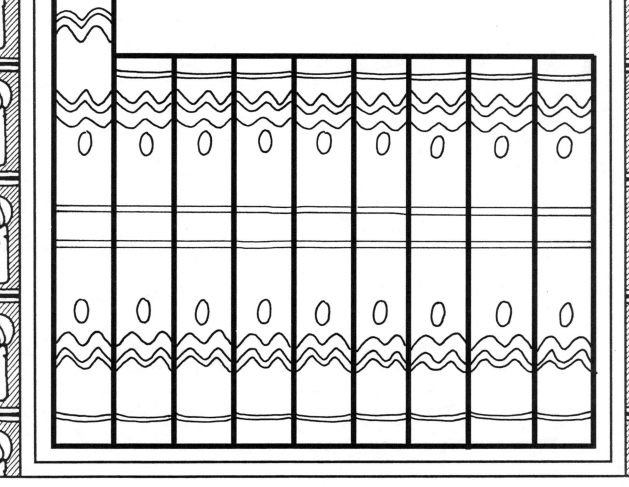

GA1429

Menorah Pattern

Color and cut out the menorah.

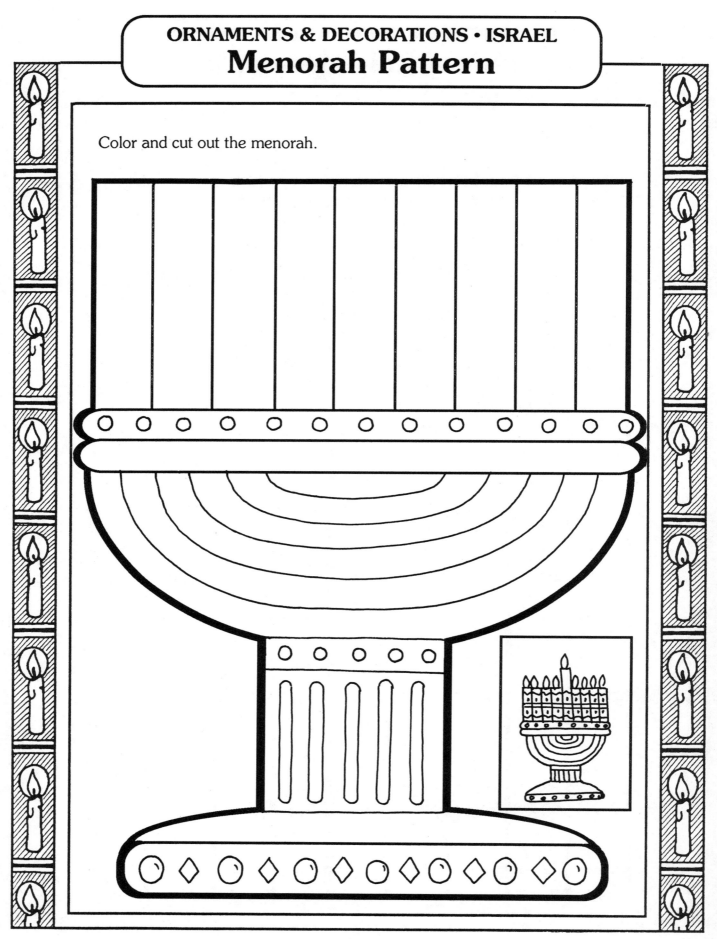

Egg Carton Dreidels

Help your students make these miniature dreidels using the pattern on this page, plastic foam egg carton cups, crayons, scissors, glue, and plastic straws or toothpicks.

1. Color, cut out, and glue a character to each side of an egg carton cup.
2. Push a pencil through the bottom of the cup to make a small hole.
3. Cut a 3" (7.62 cm) length of a plastic straw and carefully push it through the hole.
4. Use buttons, milk carton caps, or construction paper coins to play.

3" straw

ש	ה	ג	נ
SHIN	HAY	GIMEL	NUN

For a take-home gift:
1. Fold a sheet of construction paper in half.
2. Decorate the front of the card and write a holiday message.
3. Tape the finished dreidel on the front of the card.
4. Glue the playing directions inside the card.
5. Tape a pocket to the back of the card and insert yellow construction paper tokens.

To play:

1. Divide the tokens equally among players.
2. Begin play by spinning the dreidel.
3. When it stops, follow the directions for the character shown.
4. The player with all the tokens wins.

nun/nikhts = nothing   **gimel/gantz = everything**
hay/halb = half   **shin/shtell-arein = put in**

GA1429

Paper Plate Menorah

Your students will enjoy making this unique paper plate menorah to celebrate the Hanukkah season.

Provide each child with a paper plate, crayons, glue, glitter, paint or markers, strips of colored crepe paper streamers, and nine Popsicle sticks.

1. Cut a paper plate in half and decorate the outside.
2. Wrap and glue crepe paper strips to nine Popsicle sticks for candles as shown.
3. Glue candles on the curve of the plate as shown.
4. Assemble a paper plate pocket as shown.
5. Glue scraps of yellow construction paper to the top of each candle for flames.

This paper plate menorah will stand freely.

Mint Tea

End a day of dreidel playing fun with a cup of hot mint tea.

Ingredients: crushed mint leaves, tea leaves or bags

Add hot water to a pot with crushed mint leaves and tea.
Steep five minutes and pour into cups.
(To avoid burning little mouths, you may want to cool the tea by adding a cube of ice.)

Decorate paper cups with the patterns on this page.
Have children color, cut out and glue the dreidel and menorah to the sides of their cups. For a straw topper, punch a hole at the top and the bottom of one of the symbol patterns and have children lace their straws through the holes and secure with tape.

1. Color and cut out the dreidel.
2. Tape to a paper cup or punch a hole at the top and bottom for a holiday decoration.

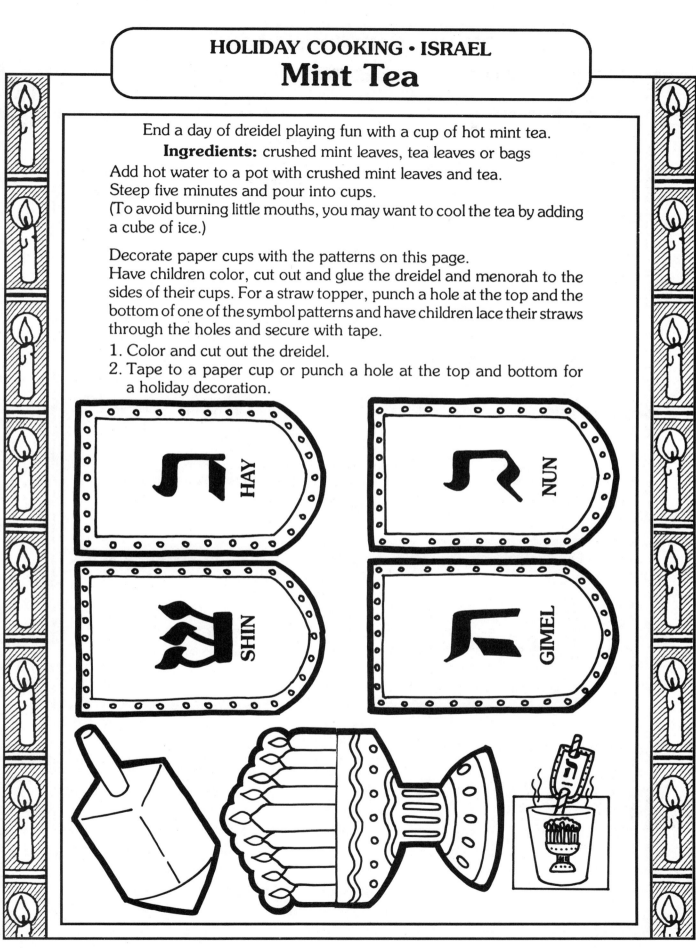

HAY

NUN

SHIN

GIMEL

GA1429

During the Christmas season tangerines and fortune cookies decorate homes and trees. And Japan's ancient god *Hoteiosho* makes an excellent substitute for Santa Claus because he has eyes in the back of his head—all the better to watch if children have been bad or good.

Besides Christmas, which is celebrated by Christians in Japan, the Japanese New Year *Kumade* is another exciting holiday which begins in mid-November and continues through December to the new year. Homemade decorations made from bamboo and orange blossoms decorate homes for the holiday season. And on the last day, New Year's Eve, families gather, share meals, and listen to the temple bells ring in the new year 108 times.

On New Year's Day children receive new games and toys such as *darumas*. Darumas are dolls which are weighted at the bottom and resemble cone-shaped beanbags. When tossed in the air they always land sitting up. Legend says that an ancient Buddist god, Dharma, sat to pray with his legs crossed for nine years. When he was done, he couldn't unfold his legs and as a result rolling was his only means of movement. And the highlight of the day is the presentation of *kakizome*, poems and proverbs written in their best handwriting.

GA1429

Parents will treasure holiday greetings from their children in their best handwriting on this keepsake scroll.

Reproduce the scroll pattern on page 54 for each child in your class and provide crayons or markers, scissors, (2) 12" (30.48 cm) dowels or plastic straws, yarn, and pencils to write special holiday greetings for the children's families. Or enlarge the scroll and have each child write his/her and her name on oaktag strips to hang on your classroom door.

1. Color and cut out the scroll.
2. Write a holiday message on the lines in your best handwriting.
3. Apply glue to the tab at the top of the scroll and attach to a dowel or straw.
4. Apply glue to the tab at the bottom of the scroll and attach to the remaining dowel.
5. Make yarn tassels as shown below to hang on either end of the bottom of the scroll.
6. Tie a length of yarn to each end of the dowel at the top of your scroll for hanging.

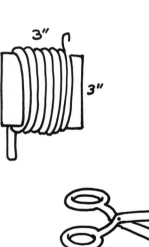

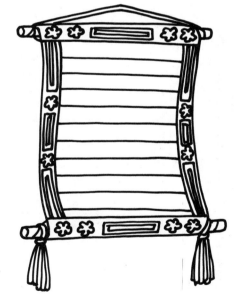

To make a tassel:
1. Cut a 3" x 3" (7.62 x 7.62 cm) square of cardboard.
2. Wrap yarn around the cardboard eight to ten times.
3. Carefully slide the wrapped yarn off the cardboard.
4. Cut a 5" (12.7 cm) length of yarn and tie it around the wrapped yarn as shown.
5. Then cut the loops at the bottom of the tassel.
6. Make two tassels and tie them to the scroll as shown.

1. Color and cut out the scroll.
2. Write a holiday message on the lines in your very best handwriting.

Apply glue here.

Apply glue here.

54

Provide your students with 12" x 18" (30.48 x 45.72 cm) sheets of construction paper, the patterns on pages 55-56, crayons or markers, scissors, and glue for delightful daruma place mats. Laminate the place mats for reuse.

For daruma place mats:
1. Decorate a sheet of construction paper.
2. Draw faces, color, and cut out the daruma dolls.
3. Arrange and glue the dolls on the construction paper.

For gift ornaments:
1. Draw faces, color and cut out the dolls.
2. Punch a hole at the top of each doll.
3. Lace and tie a length of yarn through each hole for a hanging tree ornament.

GA1429

1. Color and cut out the patterns.
2. Draw a funny face on each doll.
3. Punch a hole at the top of each doll.
4. Lace and tie a length of yarn or ribbon for a hanging ornament.

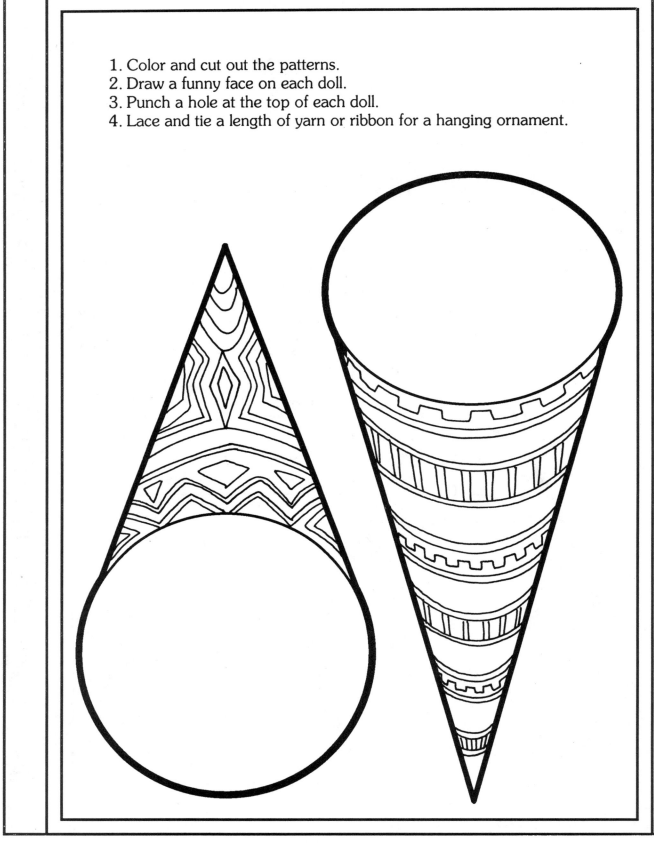

In the Philippines the celebration of Christmas begins on the 16th of December and ends on January 6, the day the Three Kings visited the Christ Child. Bells ring in this joyous holiday and tasty pastries are enjoyed by both young and old.

Colored lights decorate doorways and windows. And the *parol*, or Christmas Star, a favorite seasonal ornament often made of bamboo frames, is displayed on Christmas Eve. Making parols is a community activity. Many communities design large, elaborate parols to display in Christmas parades.

The holiday season ends on January 6, Three Kings' Day.

GA1429

Parols for the Giving

Reproduce the ornaments on pages 58-59 for each child in your class. Provide students with crayons or markers, scissors, glue, a 3 1/2" x 5 1/2" (8.87 x 13.97 cm) sheet of construction paper, and a letter-size envelope for greeting cards. For tree ornament gifts, provide students with a hole punch and yarn. (Ornaments are designed to fit in standard size envelopes.)

For greeting cards:
1. Color and cut out the patterns.
2. Fold a sheet of construction paper in half.
3. Glue a parol ornament to the cover.
4. Write a holiday message inside and sign it.
5. Insert in a decorated envelope for a holiday greeting.
6. Repeat steps 2-5 for more parol greeting cards.

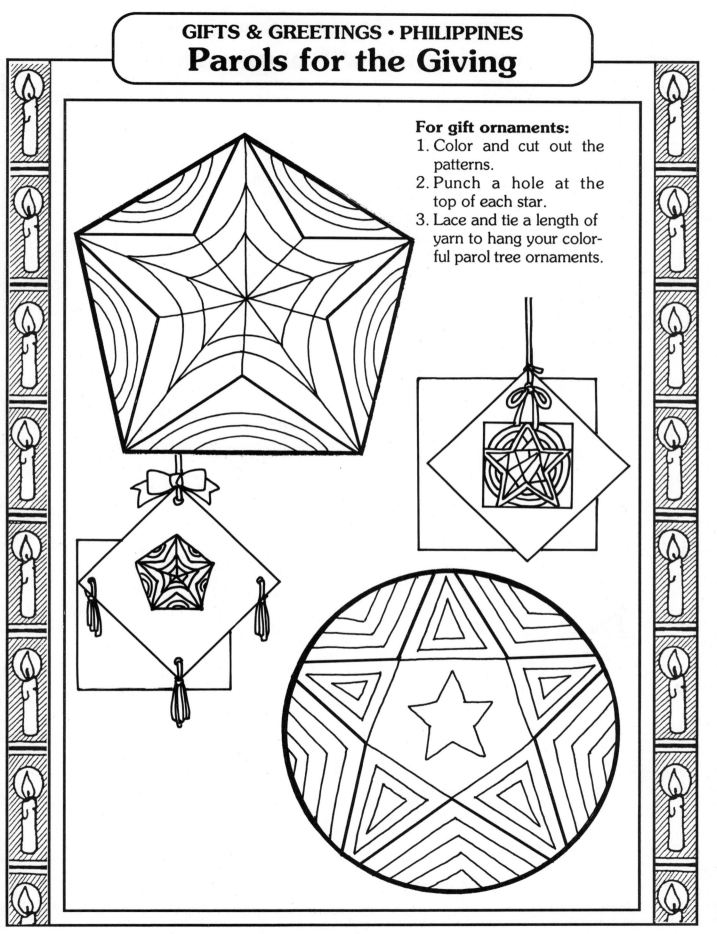

For gift ornaments:
1. Color and cut out the patterns.
2. Punch a hole at the top of each star.
3. Lace and tie a length of yarn to hang your colorful parol tree ornaments.

Your students will enjoy making this Christmas star to decorate windows in their homes.

Provide each child with the patterns on pages 60-61, the ring, a hole punch, 1" x 3" (2.54 x 7.62 cm) strips of colored crepe paper, scissors, glue, and seven 12" (30.48 cm) lengths of yarn.

1. Color and cut out the patterns.
2. Punch a hole at each dot around the *rolyo* pattern.
3. Thread and tie three lengths of yarn through one hole. Skip one hole and tie three more lengths of yarn to the next hole as shown.
4. Twist, thread, and fluff crepe paper strips through the remaining holes.
5. Glue the star to the center of the rolyo.
6. Tie a length of yarn to the top of your parol and hang in a window.

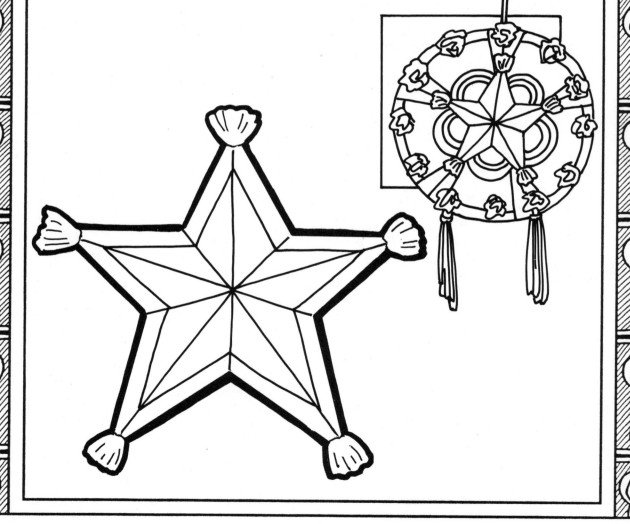

Rolyo Pattern

1. Color and cut out the pattern.
2. Punch a hole at each dot.
3. Lace and tie three lengths of yarn through two holes as shown.

GA1429

Caramel Delight

Flan, caramel custard, is one of the Filipinos' traditional holiday desserts. Substitute vanilla ice cream topped with caramel syrup and serve in student-decorated cups.

Reproduce the patterns on pages 62-63 and supply each student with crayons or markers, scissors, glue, and paper cups for a delicious holiday treat.

1. Color and cut out the pattern.
2. Glue the cup wrapper around a paper cup.
3. Then glue the stars to the cup.
4. Serve vanilla ice cream topped with caramel syrup for a tasty holiday dessert.

GA1429

1. Color and cut out the pattern.
2. Glue the pattern around a paper cup.

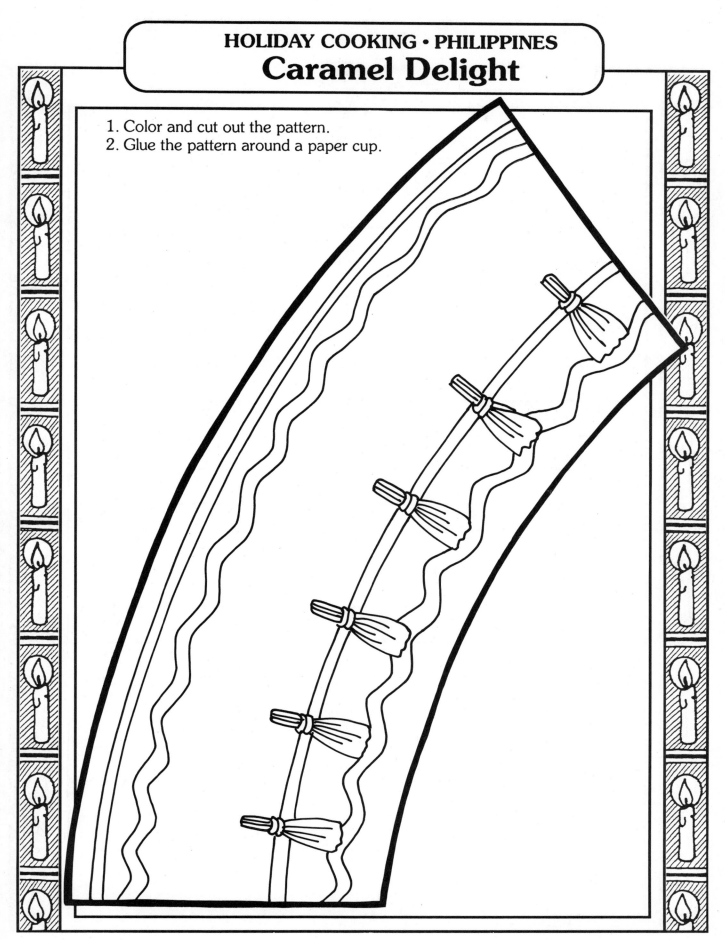

CHRISTMAS IN
Asia

_____

_____

_____

_____

_____

_____

_____

_____

_____

_____

_____

_____

_____

_____

_____

_____

_____

_____

_____

_____

_____

_____

_____

GA1429

AUSTRALIA

GA1429

Australians celebrate Christmas in their midsummer. Australia and the British Isles have similar holiday traditions, but singing carols by candlelight is an Australian tradition. This tradition began in the nineteenth century when miners gathered around lights known as "fat jacks" on Christmas Eve to sing carols. Eventually this tradition was called "Carols by Candlelight." Later, in the early, early twentieth century, a radio announcer saw an elderly lady holding a candle while singing a carol, and he initiated a campaign and succeeded in making this a nationally recognized sing-along tradition.

The "kissing bough," a traditional ornament, dates back to ancient times when mistletoe was believed to bring good luck. Today, mistletoe is still used along with a willow branch circle decorated with greenery, apples, and candles to display in homes during the Christmas holiday season.

Provide your students with the patterns on pages 67-74 to make holiday gifts, greetings, ornaments, decorations, and works of art with an Australian flavor.

GA1429

Kissing Bough Mobile

Provide your class with paper plates, scissors, yarn, green paint, a hole punch, construction paper, glue, and the patterns on pages 67-68 to make paper plate kissing bough mobiles as take-home gifts.

1. Cut out the center of a paper plate as shown.
2. Paint the plate. Allow to dry.
3. Punch six holes around the outer edge of the plate and four holes around the inner edge.
4. Color and cut out the apple and candle patterns.
5. Cut six lengths of yarn.
6. Punch a hole at the top of each apple and tie one length of yarn to each apple; then tie the other end to one of the holes around the outside of the plate.
7. Fold and glue the candles to the plate as shown.
8. Cut four lengths of yarn and tie one to each hole on the inside of the plate.
9. Now tie the fourth length in a knot as shown and hang from the ceiling or on a hanger for display.

1. Color and cut out the patterns.
2. Punch a hole at the top of each apple.
3. Fold the tab on each candle.

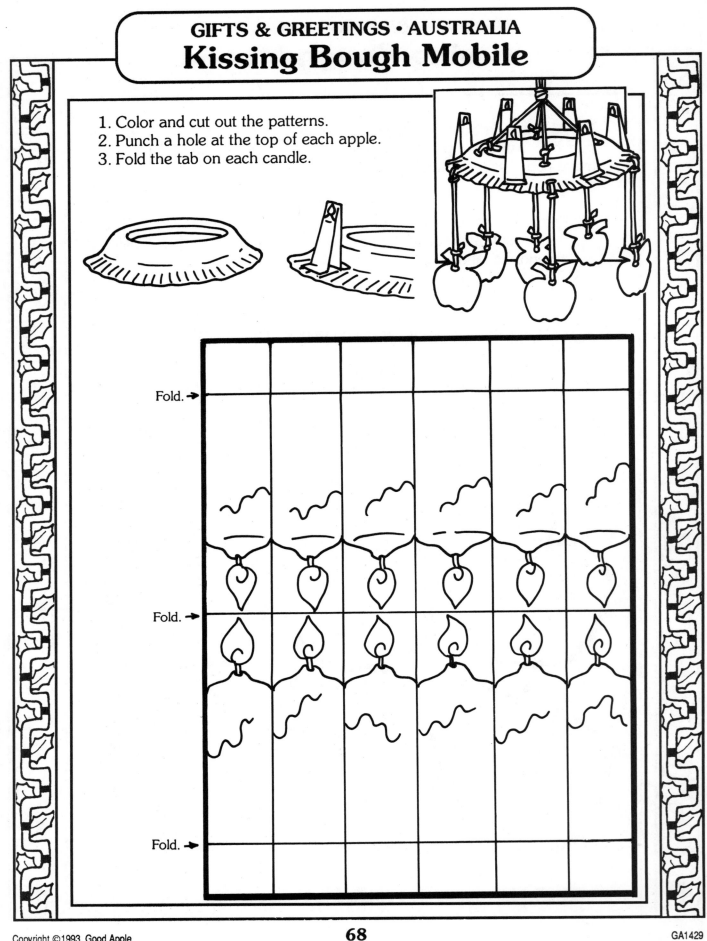

GA1429

Koalas, Swans, and "Rooz"

Your students will enjoy making homemade Christmas ornaments for gifts to friends and relatives. Provide each child with the patterns on pages 70-72, crayons, or markers, a variety of craft supplies, such as glitter, tinsel, and ribbon, scissors, construction paper, glue and yarn for these delightful holiday ornaments.

For holiday ornaments:
1. Color, decorate, and cut out the ornaments.
2. For a gift, write a holiday message on the back of each ornament.
3. Punch a hole at the top of each ornament and tie a length of yarn for hanging.

For holiday place mats:
1. Color the ornaments.
2. Cut out the ornaments excluding the hanger.
3. Decorate a 12" x 18" (30.48 x 45.72 cm) sheet of construction paper.
4. Arrange and glue the ornaments on the construction paper place mat.
5. Write a holiday message at the top.

For a holiday door decoration:
1. Color and cut out the patterns.
2. Arrange and glue the patterns to a long sheet of butcher paper or colored bulletin board paper.
3. Tie a holiday bow and glue to each ornament.

GA1429

1. Color and cut out the patterns.
2. Write a holiday message on the back.
3. Punch a hole at the top and tie a length of yarn to each ornament for hanging.

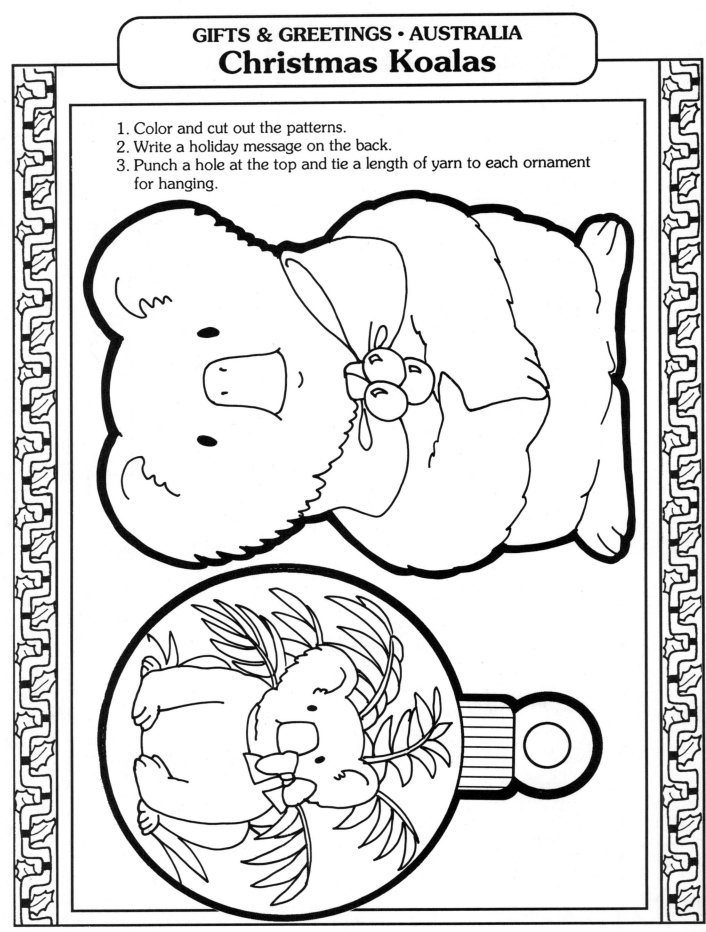

GA1429

1. Color and cut out the patterns.
2. Write a holiday message on the back.
3. Punch a hole at the top and tie a length of yarn to each ornament for hanging.

GA1429

1. Color and cut out the patterns.
2. Write a holiday message on the back.
3. Punch a hole at the top and tie a length of yarn to each ornament for hanging.

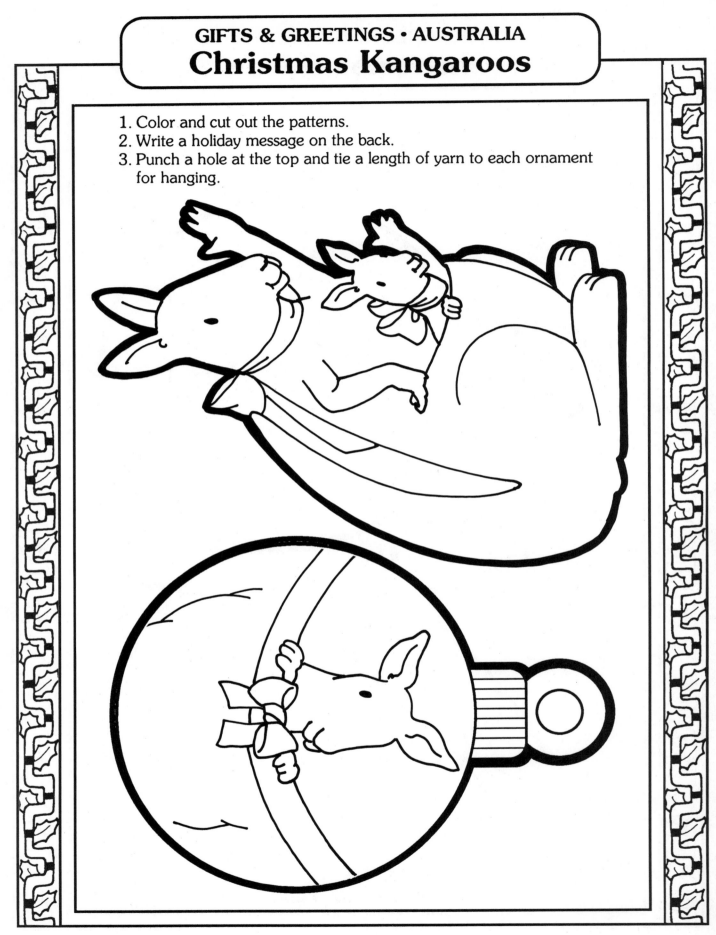

GA1429

Apple Garland

Provide your students with red, green, and yellow construction paper apples and green leaves, scissors, glue, a hole punch, yellow yarn, and gold ribbon for a bright apple garland to decorate your class tree, bulletin board, or for students to take home.

1. Color and cut out the apples and leaves.
2. Glue the leaves to the apples as shown.
3. Punch a hole on each side of the apples as shown.
4. Tie gold ribbon bows and glue to the tops of each apple.
5. Now lace the apples with a length of yarn as shown. Tie extra lengths of yarn as needed.

Color and cut out the apples.

GA1429

CHRISTMAS IN
Australia

GA1429

EUROPE

GA1429

The Christmas tree is the center of the holiday season in Austria. Traditionally the father picks out and dresses the tree with candles rather than artificial lights. Gifts, believed to have been left by Knecht Ruprecht, a jolly fellow similar to Santa Claus, are placed unwrapped under the tree. Knecht Ruprecht, like Santa, wears a long white beard, a red coat, boots, and rides in a reindeer-drawn sleigh.

Reproduce the projects on pages 78-79 for children to create Candle-Wish Trees and 3-D centerpiece trees for take-home gifts. You may want to provide your students with magazines for cutout pictures to glue on candle inserts for the Candle-Wish Tree project.

Provide each child with glue, scissors, crayons or markers, glitter pens, scraps of wrapping paper, stickers, macaroni, and construction paper to decorate their 3-D centerpiece trees.

Reproduce the tree pattern on page 79 on green construction paper and provide students with crayons or markers, scissors, glue, colored construction paper scraps, stickers, a hole punch and yarn to make this Candle-Wish Tree to display on your class bulletin board or as take-home door decorations or gifts.

1. Color and cut out the patterns.
2. Draw a simple picture of a gift you would like to receive at the end of each candle. Or, for a gift, write a special holiday message on each candle for someone special.
3. Fold the tree pattern where indicated and cut along the dotted lines to make slots for the candles.
4. Unfold the tree. Apply glue along the edges and place on a sheet of colored construction paper. Then, following the outline, cut a border around the tree as shown.
5. When dry, decorate your tree with crayons or markers, construction paper scraps and stickers.
6. Insert a candle in each slot and punch a hole at the top of the tree and tie a length of yarn for hanging.

GA1429

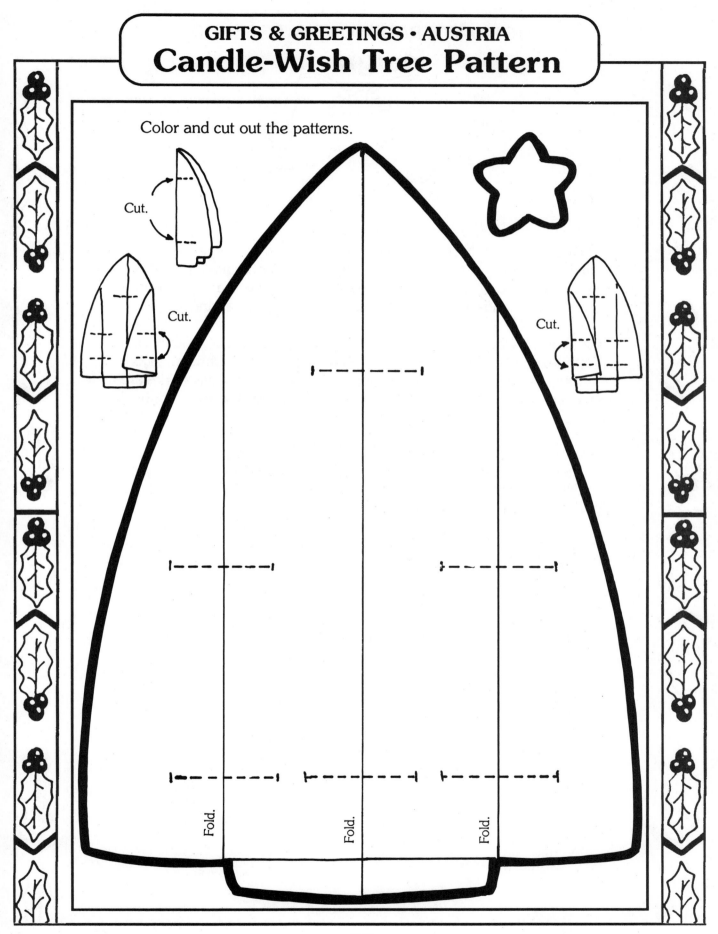

Color and cut out the patterns.

Cut.

Cut.

Cut.

Fold.

Fold.

Fold.

GA1429

The coming of St. Nicholas on December 6 marks the beginning of the children's month of holiday celebrations. However, unlike Santa Claus, St. Nicholas wears an elaborate long robe, white gloves, and a large ring on his right hand—believed to influence creatures great and small.

Children fill wooden shoes with cookies as a snack for St. Nicholas in hopes that he will fill the shoes with gifts and goodies on Christmas Day. Throughout Belgium marionette performances of Christmas stories are enjoyed by children of all ages, and midnight religious services are held everywhere.

Decorate your class bulletin board with student-decorated wooden shoe pockets on page 81 and reproduce the patterns on pages 82-84 for your students to decorate and assemble their own hinged puppets for holiday performances.

Provide students with scissors, glue, a hole punch and bright colored ribbon to make this wooden shoe holiday decoration.

1. Color and cut out the shoe.
2. Apply glue to the side and bottom edges of the shoe and attach to a 6" (15.24 cm) square of construction paper.
3. Punch a hole at the top of the square.
4. Tie a length of ribbon through the hole for hanging.
5. Fill your wooden shoes with a holiday treat for someone special.

For a greeting card:
1. Follow steps 1 and 2 above.
2. Write a holiday message on the outside of a folded sheet of costruction paper to form a card.
3. Glue the shoe inside the card.
4. Fill the shoe with cookie and candy cane-shaped construction paper goodies with a holiday message written on the back of each.

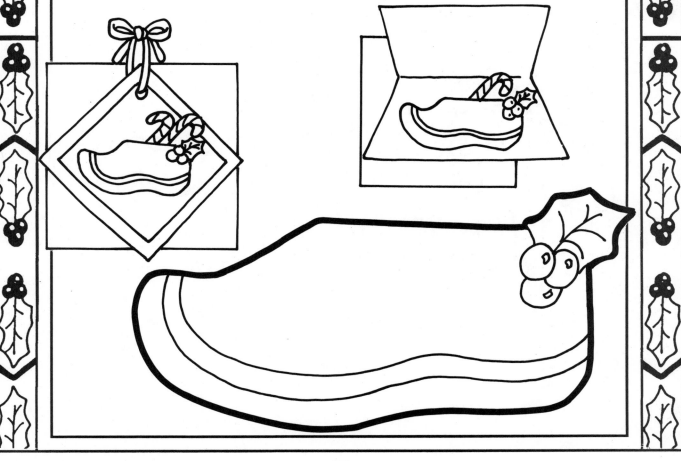

GA1429

St. Nick's Helper

Provide each child with five brad fasteners, a hole punch, crayons or markers, scissors, yarn, and the patterns on pages 82-84 to make delightful helpers to hold holiday rewards or treats.

1. Color and cut out the patterns.
2. Glue the pocket to the front of the body.
3. Punch a hole in each pattern where indicated.
4. Attach the head, arms, and legs with brad fasteners as shown.
5. Tie a length of yarn to the top of the helper to hang on a door in a window or on the class bulletin board.
6. Fill the St. Nick's helper's pocket with holiday goodies.

1. Color and cut out the patterns.
2. Glue the pocket to the front of the body.
3. Punch a hole in each pattern where indicated.

St. Nick's Helper Patterns

1. Color and cut out the patterns.
2. Punch a hole in each pattern where indicated.

84

Denmark

Christmas celebrations begin as early as October in Denmark. This is the result of holiday gifts and greetings that are sent by mail to destinations such as Tasmania and the Aleutian Isles.

In November draped fir garlands, papier-mâché bells, stars, and electric lights decorate store fronts, and the advent of Jul (Christmas) is felt throughout the country, and nissers are spied everywhere—in shop windows, on gifts, on curtains, at dinner tables, etc. A nisser is a small furry creature dressed in gray with a red bonnet. It wears long red stockings and white clogs and is believed to inhabit lofts of old farmhouses.

Your students will delight in creating a nisser invasion with the patterns on pages 86-88. Enlist the help of parent volunteers for younger children to reproduce the patterns on oaktag and provide each child with gray, red and white felt; a small, red satin bow; red buttons; construction paper; scissors; glue and a clothespin to make his own Christmas nisser.

GA1429

1. Color and cut out the patterns.
2. Trace the coat, stockings, hat and shoes onto pieces of felt.
   red stockings and hat
   gray coat
   white shoes
3. First glue the hat, coat and stockings on your nisser.
4. Then glue the shoes over the stockings.
5. Now glue a red button on the nisser's coat and a red bow under his chin.
6. When dry, glue a clothespin to the back of your nisser as shown.
7. Attach your nisser to a gift package, curtain, hat, your coat collar, or on your Christmas tree.

GA1429

Provide students with 4" (10.16 cm) construction paper circles, scissors, glue, a hole punch, and yarn.

1. Color and cut out the patterns on pages 87-88.
2. Glue each nisser on a colored construction paper circle.
3. Punch a hole at the top of each circle and tie a length of yarn for hanging.

GA1429

In Finland, Santa comes to visit in person with half a dozen elves to help distribute gifts and goodies. The elves are dressed in brown costumes, knee-length pants, red stockings and caps.

Homes are decorated with fruits, candies, paper flags, cotton, tinsel and candles, and families and friends wish each other a Merry Yule.

Decorate your class bulletin board with merry elves made by your students. Ask children to bring brown grocery bags to school. Provide each child with the patterns on pages 90-92, red construction paper stockings and caps, a hole punch and yarn to make large bulletin board good-work holders or greeting card holders to take home. Encourage children to take their elves home to decorate front doors.

Provide children with the patterns on pages 90-92, crayons or markers, red construction paper caps and stockings, glue, a hole punch and a 12" (30.48 cm) length of yarn. Enlarge the patterns for a classroom bulletin board display.

1. Color and cut out the patterns.
2. Apply glue and assemble the elf as shown.
3. Apply glue to the sides and bottom of the elf's pocket and attach to his overalls.
4. Punch two holes at the top of the elf's hat.
5. Lace and tie a length of yarn to hang your greeting card holder.
6. Punch a hole at the top of each circle and tie a length of yarn for hanging.

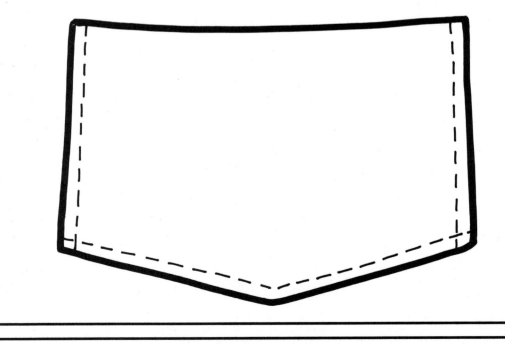

GA1429

1. Color and cut out the pattern.
2. Apply glue and assemble the elf as shown.

GA1429

1. Color and cut out the pattern.
2. Apply glue and assemble the elf as shown.

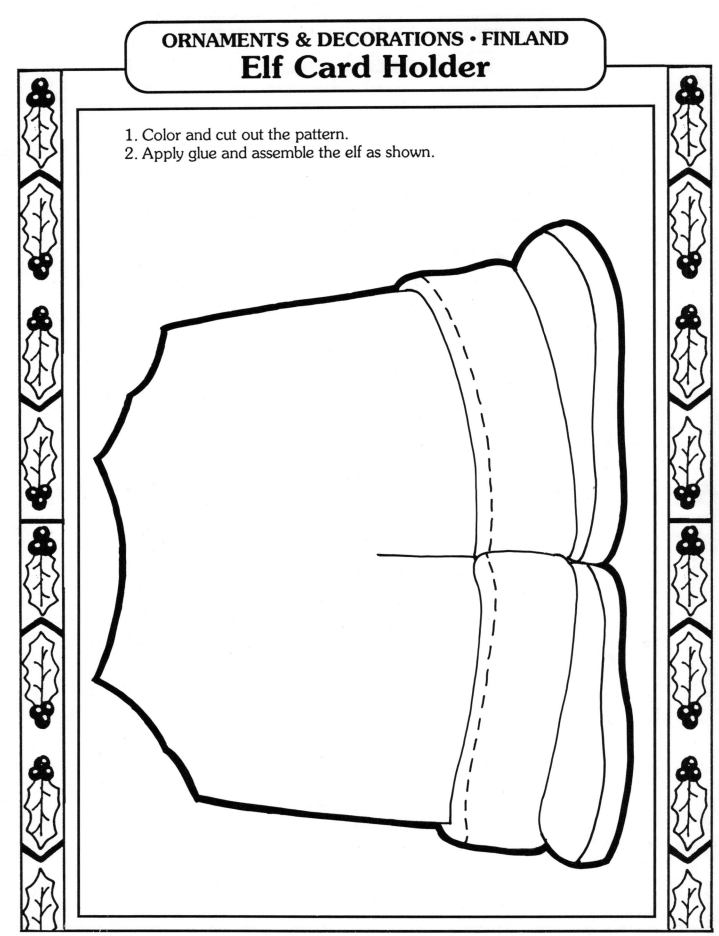

GA1429

In France, Christmas trees are rarely seen in public places. Families decorate their trees a few days before Christmas with candles and many colored stars. When the children fall asleep, small toys, sweets, and fruits are added to the trees as gifts from Santa.

Originally, on Christmas Eve, peasants would place their wooden shoes called sabots by the fireplace for Santa to leave gifts. This tradition has changed somewhat. Sabots have been replaced with chocolate shoes filled with candies.

Provide your class with the miniature ornament patterns on page 94 to make take-home tree ornaments. Ask parents to send treats to fill the sabot tree pockets for a classroom holiday treat bulletin board display.

Mini Ornaments

Provide your students with the patterns below, crayons or markers, ribbon for bows, glue, a hole punch, and yarn to make a set of miniature holiday ornaments to decorate your class tree or as an extra-special gift for their families.

1. Color and cut out the patterns.
2. Punch a hole at the top of each ornament.
3. Lace and tie a length of yarn to each for hanging.
4. Glue a festive bow to the top of each ornament.

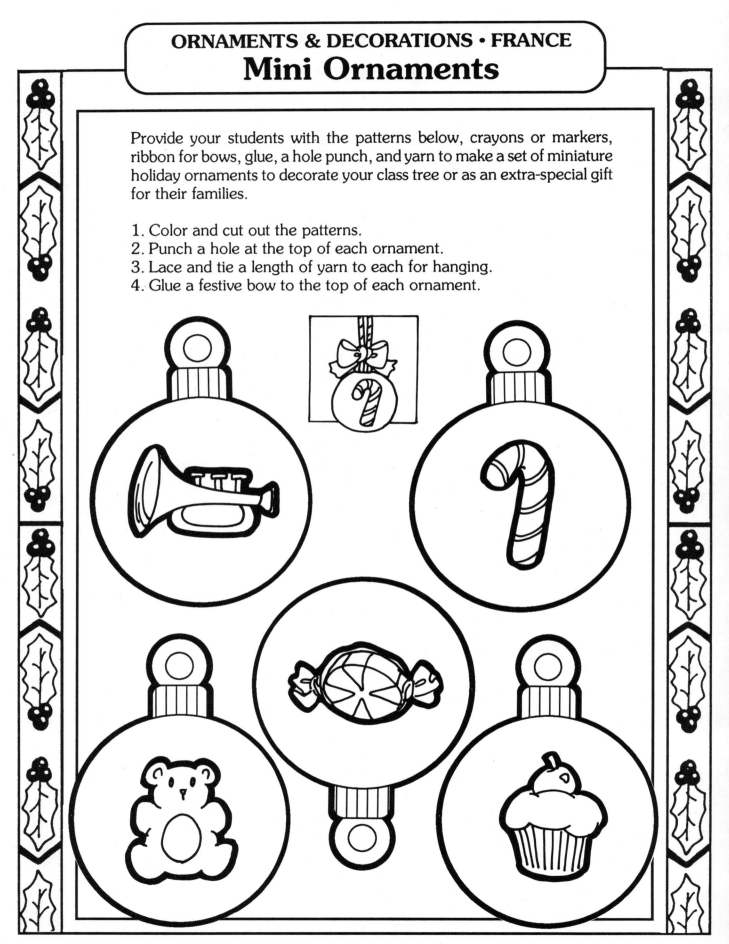

GA1429

Germans begin the season's celebrations on the Sunday nearest November 30. Advent celebrations continue until *der erste Weihnachstag*, Christmas Day. *Lichtwochen*, light weeks, are the first signs as the holiday season approaches with bright lights and home-made decorations strung from lampposts and in store fronts.

"Sugar trees" (*Christmas* or *Zuckerbaums),* trees covered with cookies, sweets, and candies, are traditional holiday decorations. Advent calendars made of cardboard with dated flaps are a favorite with children. Some calendars have pictures of holiday scenes under the flaps, words referring to the Nativity, or treats.

On December 6, as in many other countries, St. Nicholas visits homes at night and leaves small gifts of apples, nuts, and sweets for children who have been good. And families travel to large cities for the opening of the *Weihnachtsmarkt*, the Christmas market, similar to fun-filled elaborate street fairs.

Christmas Eve concludes the advent season when families gather for special suppers and children eagerly wait as adults light the tree in another room. "O Tannenbaum," an old German folk song, precludes the opening of gifts stacked on separate little tables for each member of the family from *Weihnachtmann*, Christmas Man.

GA1429

Provide crayons, glue, glitter, yarn, scissors, and a hole punch.

1. Color and cut out the pattern.
2. Fold and glue the cone as shown.
3. Decorate your cornucopia.
4. Punch a hole where indicated and tie a length of yarn for hanging.
5. Fill your cornucopia with tasty holiday treats to hang on a tree.

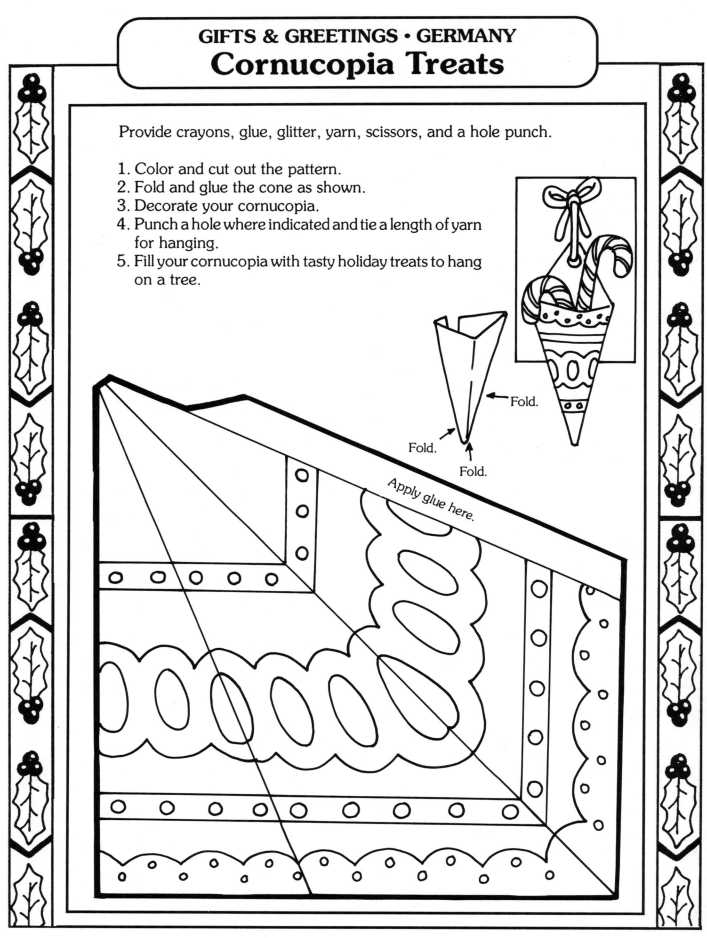

Fold.

Fold.

Fold.

Apply glue here.

GA1429

Your students will delight in making a giant Advent calendar. Encourage each child to make his or her ornament at home or secretly, during free time in class. Assign children numbers 1-25 and in turn, have them display their finished ornaments on a giant bulletin board tree.

Provide children with magazines, old greeting cards, scissors, crayons or markers, glue, and glitter.

1. Color, decorate, and cut out the pattern.
2. Cut out and glue a picture from a magazine or an old greeting card inside your ornament.
3. Write your name on the front.

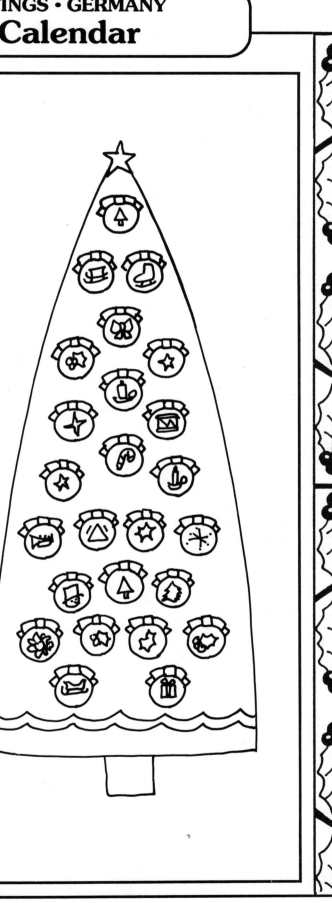

GA1429

1. Color and cut out the pattern.
2. Fold the pattern as shown.

Provide each child with a cover pattern, twenty-five blank ornament pages, crayons or markers, a hole punch, scissors, glue, yarn, and old greeting cards to make their own take-home Advent calendars.

1. Color and cut out the cover page.
2. Cut out and glue pictures from old greeting cards on each page of your Advent calendar booklet.
3. Write numbers 1-25 on the finished pages.
4. Punch two holes at the top of all the pages.
5. Bind the pages in order with a length of yarn.

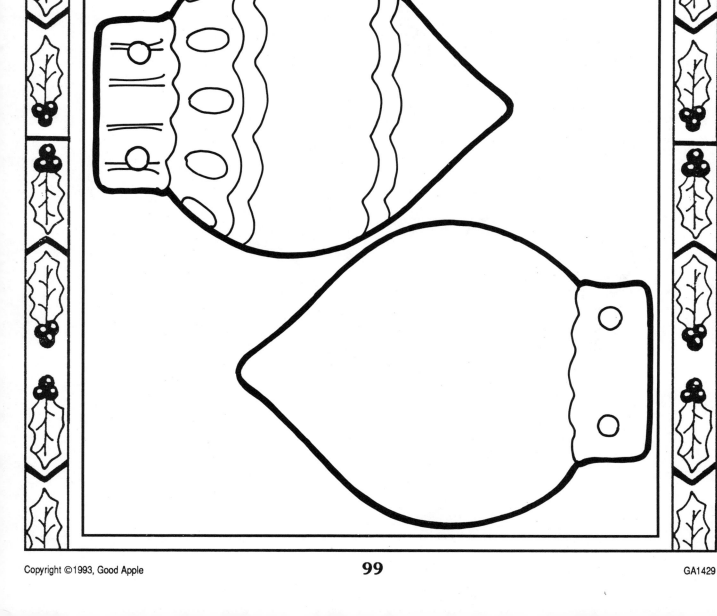

GA1429

Provide students with pink, blue or yellow tissue paper; glue; glitter; crayons or markers; and doily circles to complete this paper plate angel project.

1. Glue layers of colored tissue paper scraps on the wings.
2. When dry, color and cut out the patterns.
3. Glue the wings to the back of the angel's body.
4. Cut a doily in half and glue to the back of the angel as shown.
5. Carefully fold the angel as shown to make your angel free-standing.

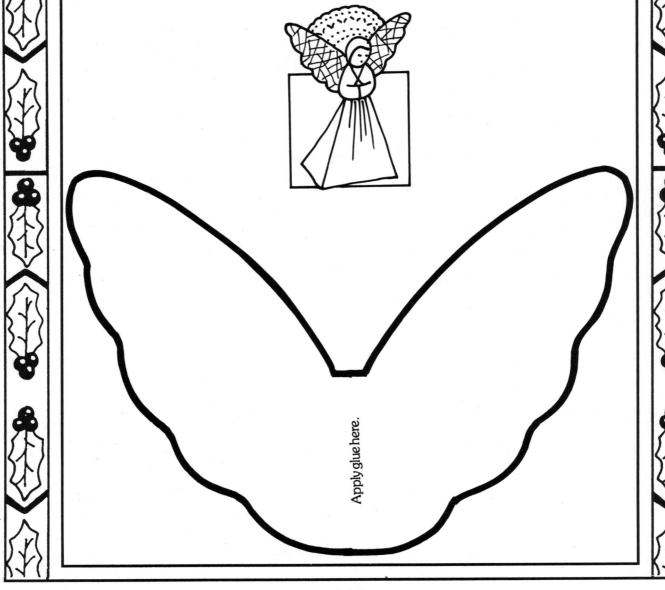

Apply glue here.

100

GA1429

Cut out the patterns.

GA1429

In Great Britain, children eagerly hang their stockings by the fireplace in hopes that Father Christmas will leave gifts and goodies to be found on Christmas Day.

Plum pudding, a traditional and favorite dish, bannock cakes, and baked oatmeal cookies are served during the holidays. *Wassail*, meaning "be thou well," is a beverage of hot ale, spices, and toasted apples.

Homes are decorated with garlands of holly and ivy; and traditional mistletoe wreaths, once considered good luck, hang in most homes.

Provide students with craft supplies to complete the project on page 103 for cookie pockets.

Use the patterns below to make individual bannock cake pockets to hang on trees, for holiday bulletin boards or as gifts. Provide students with crayons or markers, a hole punch, glue, scissors, and yarn.

1. Color and cut out the patterns.
2. Fold and apply glue to the tabs on Pattern A and attach it to Pattern B as shown.
3. Glue the ears to the back of the pocket and the bow at the top as shown.
4. Punch a hole in the top and tie a length of yarn for hanging.
5. Fill the pocket with a tasty oatmeal cookie for a friend or relative.

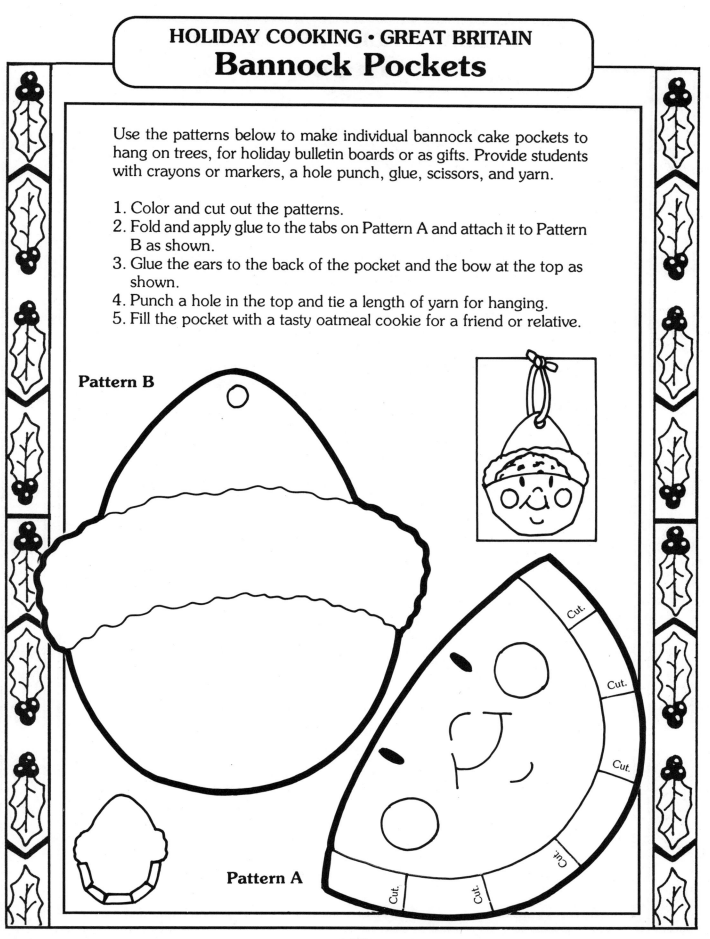

Pattern B

Pattern A

Cut. Cut. Cut. Cut. Cut. Cut.

GA1429

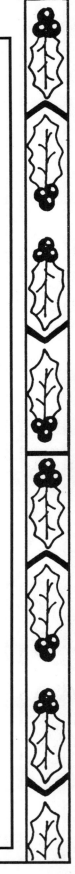

On Christmas Eve children in Greece travel through their neighborhoods in groups singing the *kalanda*, a song of the birth of the Christ Child. Other children accompany the singers by banging small metal triangles and clay drums.

Reproduce the patterns on page 105 for your students to make take-home papier-mâché decorations. Children will need paper towel rolls cut into 3" (7.62 cm) lengths, newspaper, glue, tape, paint, glitter, and yarn.

GA1429

Provide each child with three 3" (7.62 cm) towel roll tubes, newspaper strips, glue, paint, and yarn to make take-home holiday ornaments.

1. Fill the tube with newspaper and tape the ends closed.
2. Layer strips of newspaper dipped in adhesive—one part white glue, one-half part water.
3. Glue a loop of yarn on the edge of the drum as shown.
4. Reinforce the attached yarn by adding another layer of newspaper strips.
5. When the drum has dried, decorate it with paints, markers, and glitter.
6. Glue a bow to the drum as shown.

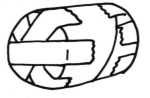

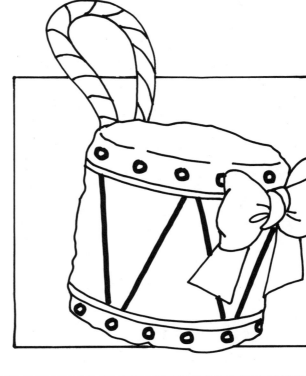

Many people believe that "Old Knick," Santa Claus, St. Nicholas, or Sinterklass originally came from Holland. His arrival on his white horse on December 5 marks the beginning of a festive holiday season.

On the eve of Sinterklass' arrival, children fill wooden shoes with straw for his horse in hopes that in the morning the shoes are filled with small gifts of sweets, topped with cookies in the shape of each child's first name.

Among other traditional holiday ornaments, children make pinwheels and string garlands of beads to decorate their homes.

Your students will enjoy making pinwheels, initial ornaments, and initial cookie baking projects on pages 107-113 to decorate your holiday bulletin board and to share with their friends and families as take-home gifts.

GA1429

Provide children with crayons or markers, glitter, scissors, glue, yarn, and Popsicle sticks to make pinwheel tree ornaments.

1. Color, cut out, and decorate the patterns.
2. Fold over and glue each corner of the pinwheel as shown.
3. Glue the medallion in place.
4. Color peppermint stripes on a Popsicle stick.
5. Attach a 6" (15.24 cm) loop of yarn to one end of the stick with glue.
6. Then apply glue to the stick and attach it to the back of the pinwheel.

Medallion

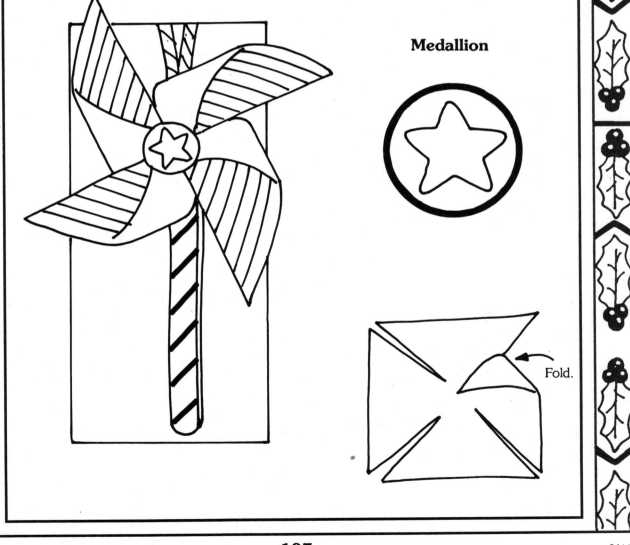

Fold.

GA1429

GA1429

Provide children with the oval pattern on this page, scissors, glue, yarn, a hole punch, and each of his or her choice of initials from pages 110-112 to make initial ornaments for friends and relatives.

1. Cut out and punch a hole at each dot around the oval.
2. Lace the oval with colorful yarn as shown. Begin and end at the top and tie the loose ends for hanging.
3. Color and cut out initials for friends and relatives.
4. Glue an initial in the center of the oval.
5. Write a holiday message and sign your name on the back.

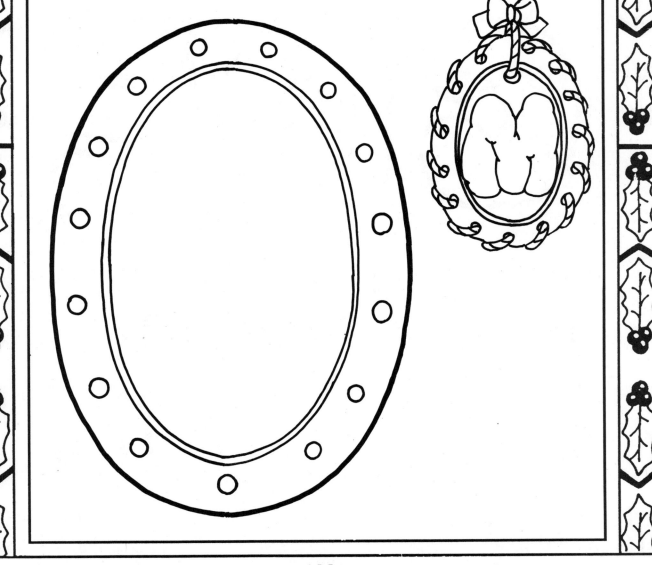

GA1429

GA1429

GA1429

GA1429

Initial Cookies

Your students will enjoy making these delightful initial cookies for each other, and as take-home gifts for their families. Enlist the help of parent volunteers to complete this holiday cooking project.

Ingredients:

prepackaged cookie dough	plastic straw
waxed paper	ribbon or yarn
gift label	

1. Cut 1" (2.54 cm) slices from prepackaged cookie dough.
2. On a sheet of waxed paper, roll a slice of dough as shown.
3. Shape the cookie roll into an initial.
4. Use a plastic straw to make a hole at the top of your initial-shaped cookie. Make sure the hole is large enough to allow for shrinkage in baking.
5. Bake per instructions on packaging. Allow to cool.
6. Color, cut out and write a holiday message on a label.
7. When the cookies are done, lace and tie a length of yarn or ribbon through the hole in the cookie and label.

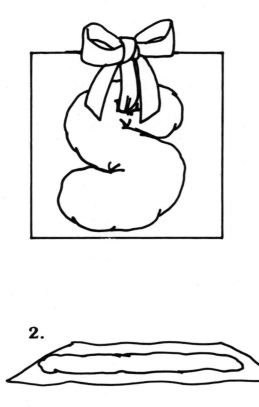

1.

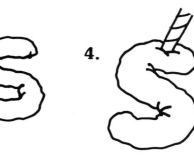

2.   3.   4.

GA1429

Christmas is traditionally a family affair in Italy. Families and close friends gather to celebrate the holiday and share in the spirit of the season. Nine evenings of religious celebrations mark the beginning of the holiday season.

Decorations include presepios, a manger and Nativity scene and sprigs of holly; mistletoe; candles; and a ceppo, Italy's version of a Christmas tree, decorated with ornaments and gifts for the family.

The *ceppo*, a word used to describe the trunk of the yule log, has changed its appearance and meaning over time. Originally it was a log brought in from the woods and set afire to be battled with by blindfolded children and adults for wishes to be heard when struck. When the blindfold was removed, gifts magically appeared. Today, ceppos are pyramid shapes trimmed with colored papers, gold and silver foil, candles, and pinecones, with shelves to display gifts.

Gift-giving day varies between regions. In some areas gifts are given on December 6, St. Nicholas Feast Day; in others gifts are received on December 13, St. Lucia's Day. In other regions a visit from Santa Claus brings gifts on December 24, and on Christmas Day a kind old man called Babbo Natale visits with gifts for children. January 6, however, is widely accepted as gift-giving day by many. On this day, the Epiphany, a kind old woman, Befana, fills children's shoes with treats.

A delightful tradition for children and parents alike is the writing of "Christmas letters." On Christmas Eve children write letters to their parents promising to be good and wishing their parents a happy holiday. The letters are then secretly placed under the father's dinner plate to be read to the entire family.

Use the patterns on pages 115-117 for family sharing gifts.

Holiday Hands

Parents will treasure these holiday hands from their children. Provide children with colored construction paper, a hole punch, ribbon, and crayons or markers.

1. Cut out the patterns.
2. Write a message on one hand.
3. Decorate the remaining hand with crayons, markers, scraps of tissue, paper, or glitter.
4. Punch two holes at the top of each hand where indicated.
5. Lace and tie a length of yarn or ribbon through the holes and tie the ends into a bow.

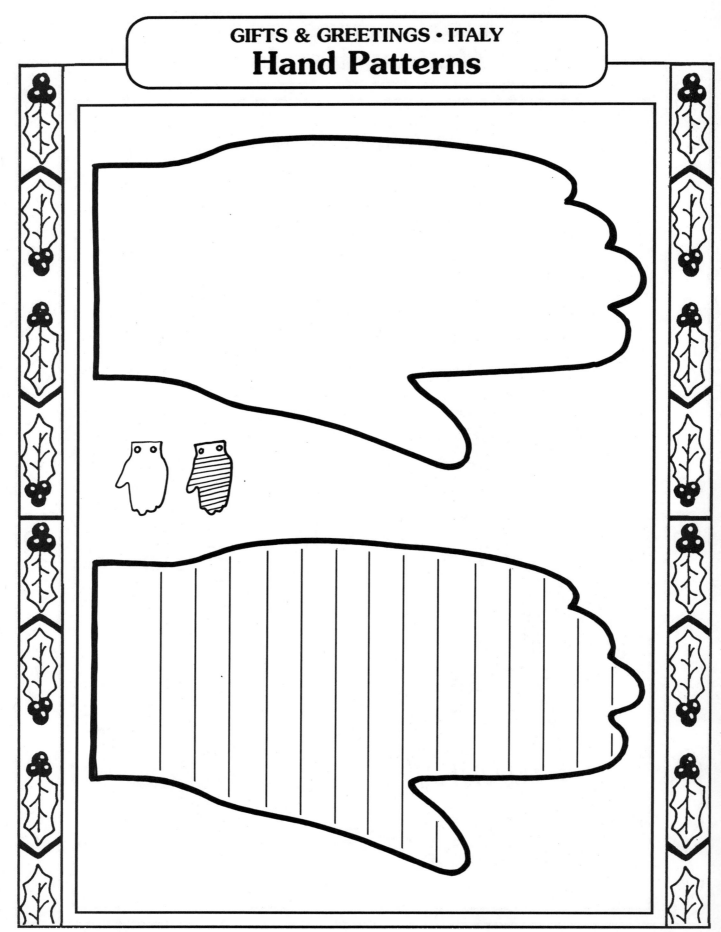

GA1429

Provide ribbon, scissors, glue, yarn, holiday pictures from magazines or old greeting cards, and these patterns for holiday ornaments.

1. Color, cut out and assemble the patterns as shown.
2. Cut out holiday pictures from magazines or old Christmas cards and glue them in the center of each triangle.
3. Punch a hole at the top of each triangle.
4. Lace and tie a length of yarn to the top of each ornament for hanging.

GA1429

Santa, gift giving, religious ceremonies, and decorating are traditional holiday customs in Spain, but the Urn of Fate is uniquely their own.

Folded slips of paper with the name of each member at the gathering of family and friends are placed in the urn. In turn, each person draws a slip from the urn and he or she is said to become best friends with the person named on the slip for the coming year. This continues until all the slips are drawn.

Reproduce the folding name tag on page 120 for a holiday season best friends activity. Encourage best friend pairs to work together to write a holiday poem or original story to display on the class bulletin board. (Make sure each pair completes two copies of their work for each to take home.)

GA1429

Color and cut out this pattern to attach to the front of a paper sack or a large cereal box for a best friend name drawing activity.

Provide each child with a Best Friend Name Tag to fill out and drop in the Urn of Fate. In turn, children draw folded name tags from the urn and the child whose name appears on the tag will be his or her best friend for a predetermined time period. Have children wear their best friend name tags during this time.

Provide each child with a name tag pattern, scissors, and crayons or markers. (If there are an uneven number of students in your class, fill out a name tag yourself and add to the drawing.)

1. Color and cut out the name tag.
2. Cut the slits on each flower.
3. Write your name inside.
4. Fold the name tag as shown and drop it in the Urn of Fate for a best friend name drawing activity.

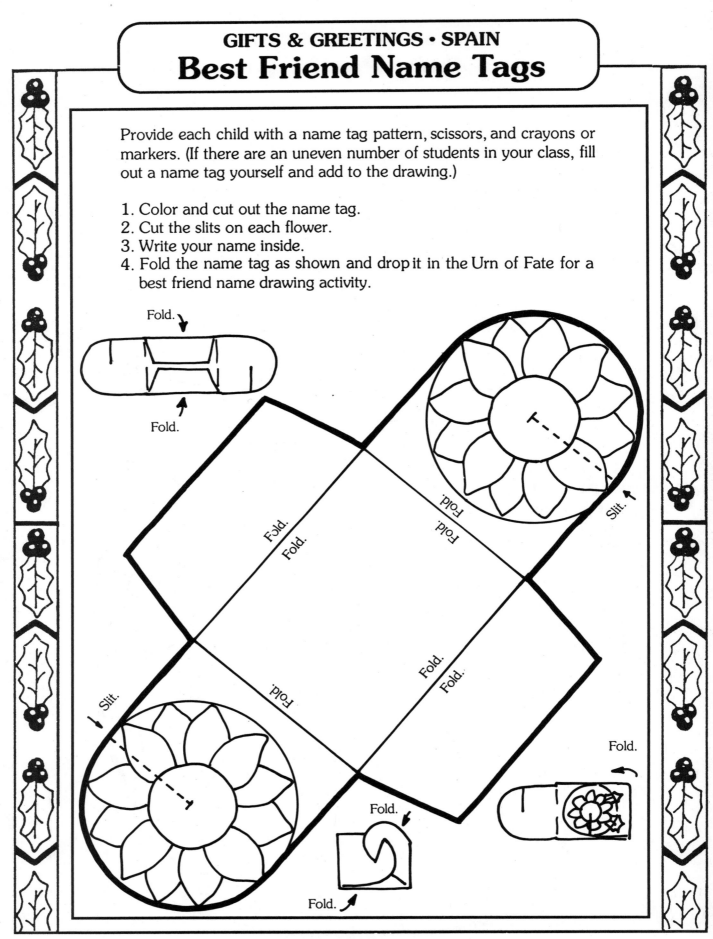

GA1429

1. Color and cut out the pattern.
2. Write a holiday poem or story on the urn.
3. Punch two holes at the top of the urn.
4. Lace and tie a length of yarn through the holes to display.

GA1429

December 13, the day chosen to commemorate the life of St. Lucia, marks the beginning of the Christmas holiday celebrations. St. Lucia, a young girl, wore a wreath with seven candles on her head to light the way through dark tunnels where Christians hid as a result of persecution.

The spirit of this event is still present during the holiday season. On the 13th the eldest daughter dresses in a white gown with a red sash, and she wears a seven-candle wreath to light the way as she carries coffee and buns to members of the family in each room. Male children accompany her, wearing tall silver paper hats and carrying silver stars.

Another traditional holiday activity is the making of straw ornaments, symbolic of the straw in the manger where the Christ Child was placed.

Use the patterns on pages 123-126 to make candle wreath headbands and lattice gifts and ornaments.

Reproduce the patterns on page 124 on brown construction paper and provide children with 1/2" (1.25 cm) yellow construction paper strips, scissors, glue, and red or green sheets of construction paper to make a set of coasters for take-home gifts. Laminate the coasters for durability.

For a coaster:
1. Cut the patterns apart and fold one pattern in half as shown.
2. Cut along the dotted lines.
3. Unfold the pattern and weave yellow construction paper strips as shown.
4. Trim excess strips to the outline of the pattern; then apply a dot of glue under each strip and secure.
5. When the glue is dry, cut out the pattern.
6. Glue the pattern in the center construction paper circle or square for a festive coaster.
7. Repeat steps 1-6 for the remaining patterns.

For a woven ornament:
1. Follow steps 1-5 listed above.
2. Glue a construction paper bow at the top. Punch a hole and tie a length of yarn for hanging.

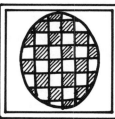

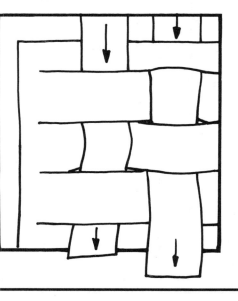

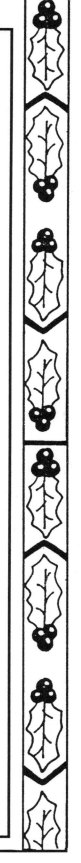

Fold and cut slits.

"Straw" Coaster Patterns

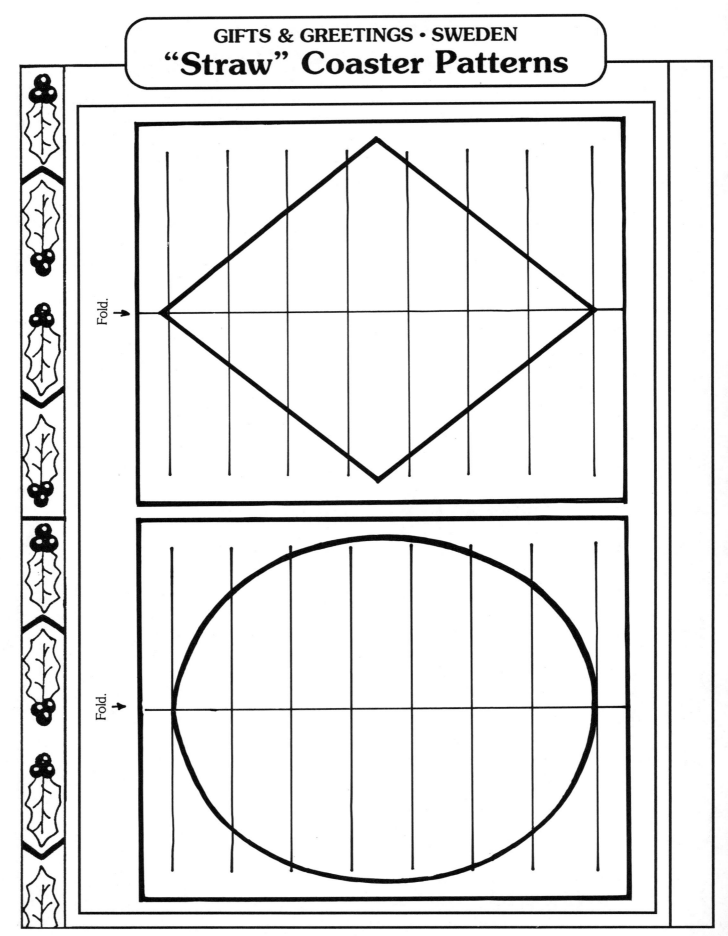

Fold.

Fold.

124

Candle Wreath Headband

1. Color and cut out the patterns.
2. Glue the ends of the headband strips together.
3. Measure and adjust the size and glue the opposite ends together to form a headband.
4. Glue the holly leaves, berries, and candles around the headband as shown.

GA1429

Candle Wreath Headband

1. Color and cut out the patterns.
2. Glue the ends of the headband strips together.
3. Measure and adjust the size and glue the opposite ends together to form a headband.
4. Glue the holly leaves, berries, and candles around the headband as shown.

126

New Year's Day is celebrated in Russia (formerly U.S.S.R.). It's the day *D'yed Moroz,* Grandfather Frost, brings holiday gifts. He wears a white beard, red robe and hat trimmed with white fur, and is accompanied by the Snow Maiden.

Popular gifts among the children of Russia are matrioskas, six identical nesting dolls. Reproduce the patterns on pages 129-132 for your students to make two-dimensional nesting dolls as holiday door decorations or gifts to give to family members or friends.

Each child will need a 30" (76.2 cm) length of bright colored yarn, the patterns on pages 129-132, craft supplies such as glitter, crayons or markers, scissors, glue, and ribbon. Encourage students to write holiday messages on the back of each doll.

Provide each child with the directions below, a 30" (76.2 cm) length of yarn, a 6" x 9" (15.4 x 22.86 cm) envelope, glitter, glue, crayons or markers, ribbon, six buttons, scissors and the patterns on pages 129-132 to complete this delightful nesting doll mobile.

1. Color and decorate the dolls.
2. Fold and glue each doll as shown.
3. Punch a hole at the top of each doll and tie a length of yarn through the hole.
4. Punch another hole in the back of the doll, at the bottom, and tie another length of yarn.
5. Tie the dolls together as pictured.
6. Attach a ribbon bow to the top of the largest doll.
7. The dolls will nest inside each other to fit in a 6" x 9" (15.24 x 22.86 cm) envelope for a holiday gift.

GA1429

Fold.

Apply glue here.

Fold.

Fold.

Fold.

GA1429

Fold.

Apply glue here.

Fold.

Fold.

Fold.

GA1429

Apply glue here.

Fold.

Fold.

Fold.

Apply glue here.

Fold.

Fold.

GA1429

Apply glue here.

Fold.

Fold.

Fold.

Apply glue here.

Fold.

CHRISTMAS IN
Europe

133

NORTH AMERICA

GA1429

Steeped in holiday traditions from many cultures, North Americans celebrate Christmas in many different ways. Regardless of unique religious and cultural differences, the spirit of Christmas, joy, goodwill, and family togetherness are ever present through the season.

Many families celebrate the holiday season with traditions and customs of their ancestors taking on an old world flavor, while some are distinctly customized celebrations combining new customs with traditional winter holidays.

In many North American regions, luminaries, small sand-filled paper bags with candles nested inside, light December nights. Some believe that this custom originated in Mexico where paper lanterns, farolitas, were carried during the nights of posadas.

Decorating and displaying Christmas trees with origins in German heritage, and the display of the Flor de la Noche, (the poinsettia) a Mexican plant introduced to North America by Joel Poinsett, are two accepted traditional Christmas customs. And then there's Santa Claus, a modern-day product of Germany's Christkindel, the Dutch Sinterklaas, and St. Nicholas, enlivened by a gentleman and scholar of New York, Clement Moore in his ballad "'Twas the Night Before Christmas."

GA1429

In Bethlehem, Pennsylvania, Moravians bake Christmas cakes and ornamental wafer-thin, ginger cookies from recipes handed down through generations. The unique holiday celebration of Christmas Lovefeast, primarily for children, is a candlelight service of music performed on Christmas Eve.

In Canada, people begin to prepare for this joyous holiday season as in other parts of the world by making or buying gifts and wrapping them in brightly colored paper and ribbons. Homes are decorated with lights and Christmas trees and créches, Nativity scenes, are displayed.

Hawaiians greet the "Christmas Tree Ship" carrying fir trees from the continental United States, and Santa arrives in a canoe.

New Englanders decorate with candles in windows.

The Pennsylvania Dutch string popcorn and cranberries to drape on Christmas trees, decorate carefully blown eggshells with strips of colored paper, and youngsters leave hats, baskets, and stockings for presents left by Krischkindel or Kindlein, the Christ Child.

Puerto Ricans celebrate *Felices Pascuas*, Happy Christmas. Christmas Eve, *Noche Buena*, marks the beginning of the holiday celebrations on this tropical island. On Christmas Day families and friends gather to share festive meals of arroz con pollo, rice and chicken, or roasted pig. On January 5, the eve of Three Kings' Day, children leave boxes under their beds for the kings to fill with gifts. (The boxes are filled with grass with cups of water for the camels to eat and drink.)

In the United States, African Americans celebrate *Kwanzaa,* a contemporary celebration of African harvest festivals. This celebration originated during the civil rights movement in the 1960's to educate African American families about their heritage.

The celebration begins on December 26 and handmade decorations of black, red, and green paper ornaments decorate each home. During Kwanzaa, families and friends gather to exchange gifts and light the *kinara,* a seven-hole candelabrum with black, red, and green candles. Each candle symbolizes one of the seven principles of Kwanzaa—unity, self-determination, work and responsibility, cooperative economics, purpose, creativity and faith.

On the first night, a child lights the black candle and places it in the center of the kinara. This lighting ceremony continues six nights. On the last night December 31, children receive *zawadi,* small gifts of books and symbols of their heritage such as African art objects.

GA1429

Egg Cup Kinara

Reproduce the pattern below for each student to design and decorate desktop or take-home gift kinaras. Provide each child with a 2" x 12" (5.08 x 30.48 cm) corrugated cardboard; 1 1/2" x 5" (3.79 x 12.7 cm) construction paper for candles–one black, three each of red and green; seven egg carton cups; paint; crayons or markers; scissors; glue; tape; and scraps of yellow tissue paper.

1. Carefully punch a hole in the bottom of each egg carton cup with a pencil.
2. Paint the cups.
3. Color and cut out the medallions.
4. Glue two medallions to each cup on opposite sides.
5. Glue the cups to the cardboard strip, side by side.
6. Using a pencil, loosely roll and tape the black candle.
7. Tear a scrap of yellow tissue paper, apply a spot of glue and insert in the candle.
8. On the first day of Kwanzaa place the black candle in the center of your kinara.
9. Repeat steps 6-7 for each remaining candle to place in your kinara for six days.

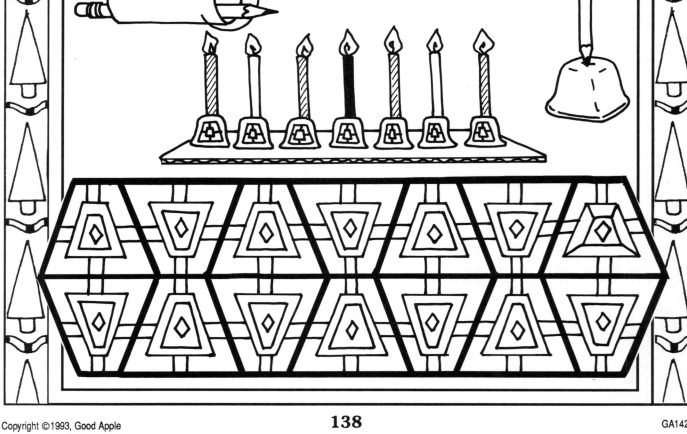

138

GA1429

The Christmas Tree Ship

Provide your students with crayons or markers, green construction paper trees, scissors, tape, and crayons or markers. Encourage children to write special notes to members of their families or friends, or list free chores on each tree as gifts to parents or siblings.

1. Color and cut out the pattern.
2. Tape the ship together as shown.
3. Write a special holiday message on a tree for each relative in your family.
4. Place the trees in the ship's pocket and display in your home during the holidays.

GA1429

The Christmas Tree Ship

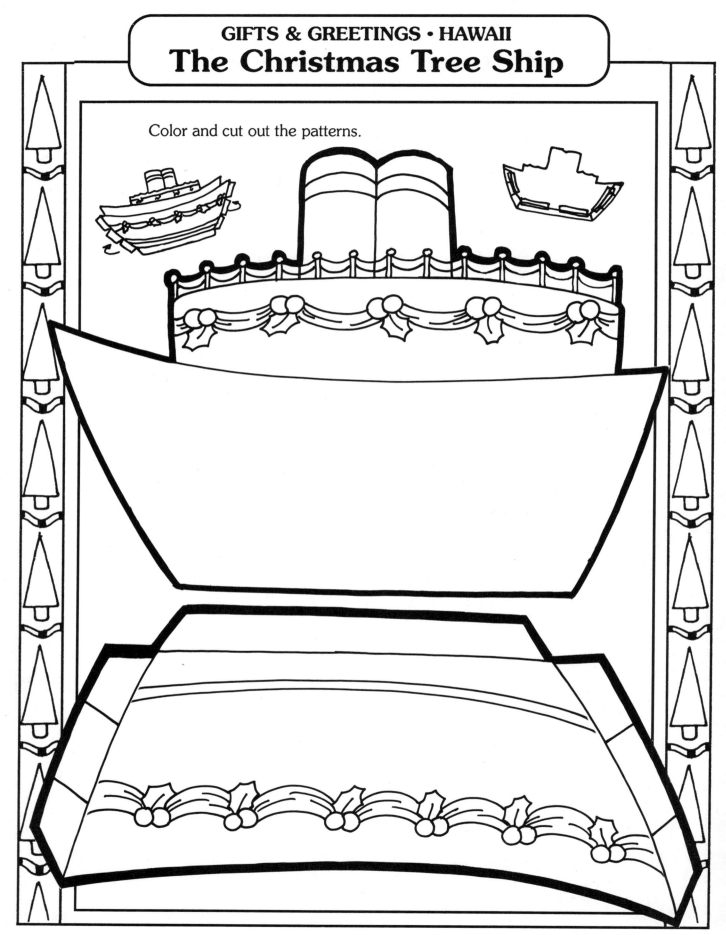

Color and cut out the patterns.

140

GA1429

In Mexico, *Navidad* (Christmas) begins with a nine-day custom called *posadas*. The English translation for a posada is "a lodging." This custom symbolizes the journey of Joseph and Mary to Bethlehem and their long search for shelter.

Families and friends go from house to house until a home chosen during the planning of these nine nights welcomes and gives them shelter. After a small religious ceremony, festivities begin. The piñata, a game centered around an elaborately decorated papier-mâché jug filled with treats, is a favorite tradition for children of all ages.

Unlike in North America, Mexicans practice gift giving on Epiphany, January 6, the day when the Magi, delivered gifts to the Christ Child. On the eve of Epiphany, children in other countries prepare for the return of the Three Kings by leaving their shoes filled with grass for the camels in hopes that they will leave gifts, but in Mexico children write letters to the Magi of their good deeds and include lists of gifts they would like to receive.

GA1429

Papier-Mâché Piñatas

Originally the piñata symbolized a combat to destroy evil. Today it is a game traditionally played at the end of each posada during Navidad. The piñata was a decorated jug made of clay. Today piñatas are elaborately decorated papier-mâché shapes–Santa Claus, animals, or snowmen– filled with treats. To play, blindfolded children take turns trying to break the piñata with a stick to make it pour holiday goodies and treats.

Enlist the help of parent volunteers for this piñata project and provide your students with a balloon, yarn, newspaper strips, four paper cups, crepe paper streamers, paint, tape, a bowl, and a solution of one part glue to one part water for an adhesive.

1. Blow up and tie a knot in your balloon.
2. Dip newspaper strips in glue solution and wrap the strips in layers around the balloon, leaving the knot visible. Allow to dry.
3. Tape the cups to the balloon as shown.
4. Dip newspaper strips in glue solution and wrap the cups. Add an extra layer over the taped intersection.
5. Cut a 3" (7.62 cm) hole around the knot. (This will burst the balloon.)
6. Then apply another layer of newspaper strips around the cut edge to reinforce the opening. Allow to dry.
7. Paint and decorate the balloon and the cups. Allow to dry.
8. Cut 6" (15.24 cm) lengths of crepe paper and glue them to the end of each cup.
9. Punch three holes around the cut-away opening and tie a length of yarn to each hole. Then tie the three lengths in a knot.
10. Fill your piñata with holiday treats and hang it.

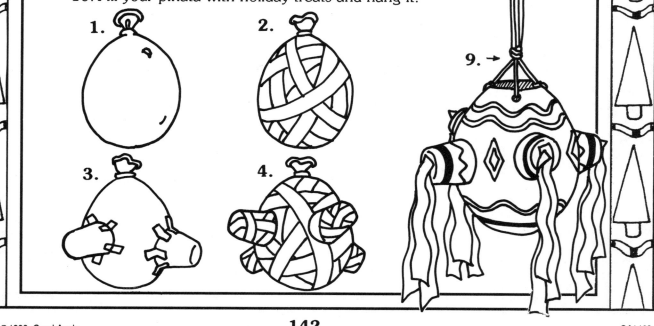

GA1429

Supply your students with the patterns on pages 143-144, crayons or markers, scissors, glue, and candy canes or other holiday treats for ornaments to display on your classroom tree, or for a bulletin board secret piñata pals display.

For tree ornaments:
1. Color and cut out the piñata pockets.
2. Apply glue to the sides and fold each pocket.
3. When dry, insert a holiday treat in the pocket for someone special.

For secret piñata pals bulletin board treats:
Using green and brown construction paper, design and post a large tree on your bulletin board. Use strips of holiday wrapping paper and red bows for the border and display Secret Piñata Pals at the top.

Have children follow steps 1-3. Then have each child write his name on a strip of paper and drop it in a paper bag. Each child draws a name from the bag and secretly writes that name on the front of the piñata pocket and his own name on the back. When each child is done, have him pin his secret pal's treat on a branch of the bulletin board tree.

Fold up.

GA1429

1. Color and cut out the piñata pockets.
2. Apply glue to the sides and fold each pocket.
3. When dry, insert a holiday treat in the pocket and write a holiday message on the back for someone special.

Trudy

Fold up.

GA1429

Ask children to bring two clean aluminum pie tins to school for this attractive candle ornament project. Enlist the help of parent volunteers for young students to help with cutting pie tins.

Provide each child with scissors, a sharp tool such as a toothpick or large paper clip, a votive candle, and the patterns on pages 145-146.

1. Design and draw a pattern of dots on each pattern where indicated.
2. Cut out and tape the patterns in the center of two pie tins.
3. Using a sharp tool, punch holes through the tin following your design.
4. Then cut the pie tin following the shape of each pattern.
5. Bend and assemble the candle holder patterns as shown on page 146.
6. Insert a candle in your candle holder for an attractive holiday display.

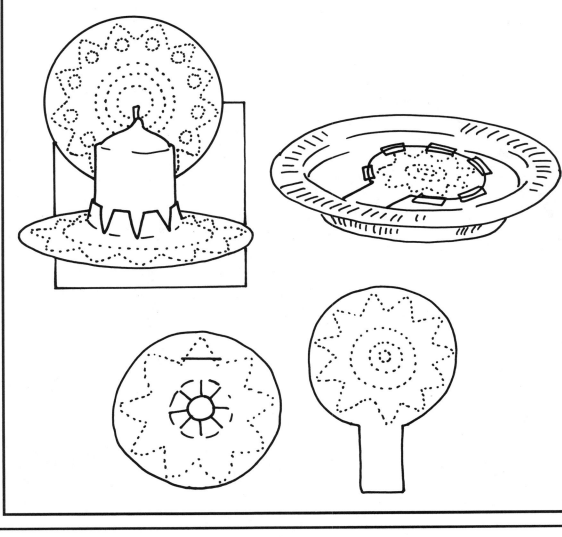

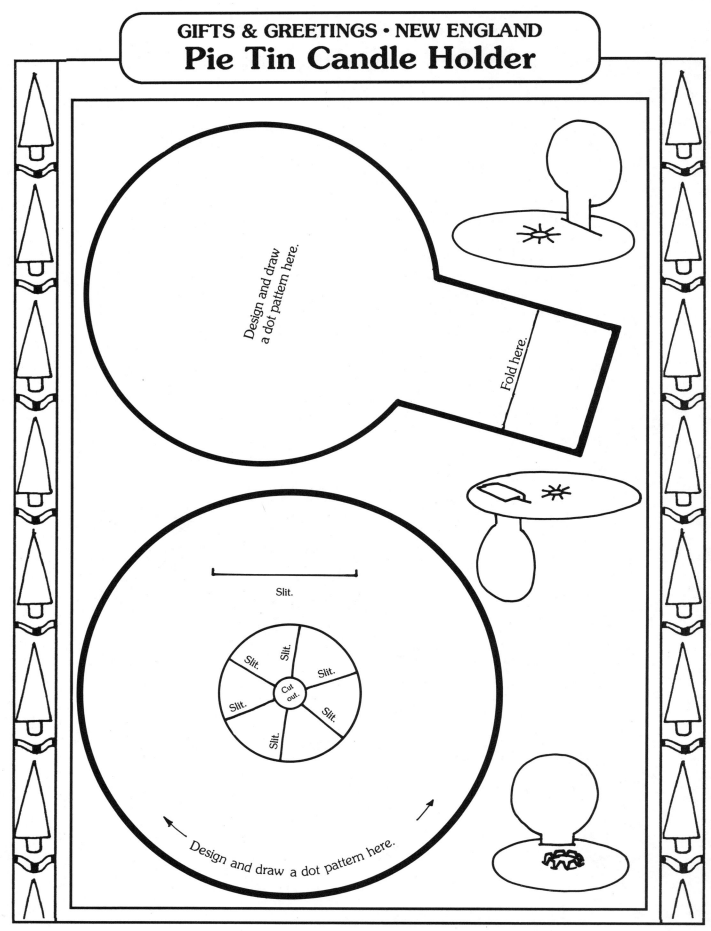

Design and draw
a dot pattern here.

Fold here.

Slit.

Slit.

Slit.

Slit.

Slit.

Slit.

Slit.

Cut
out.

Design and draw a dot pattern here.

GA1429

Children will enjoy making popcorn and cranberry garlands in class. Recruit parent volunteers to donate popcorn, cranberries, and extra hands to complete this project.

Or reproduce the patterns below and have children lace yellow construction paper popcorn and red cranberry garlands on bright colored ribbon to display in the classroom or to decorate the school auditorium for a holiday performance.

1. Cut out the patterns.
2. Lace the popcorn and cranberry patterns on a length of ribbon as shown. Tie ribbons together as needed.

GA1429

Have children bring shoe boxes to school for this project. Provide students with wallpaper scraps, gift wrap, colored construction paper, glitter, glue, scissors, crayons and markers to make their own take-home Christmas boxes to be filled with grass for the camels on the eve of Epiphany.

1. Decorate your box.
2. Write your name inside the box.

GA1429

CHRISTMAS IN
North America

SOUTH AMERICA

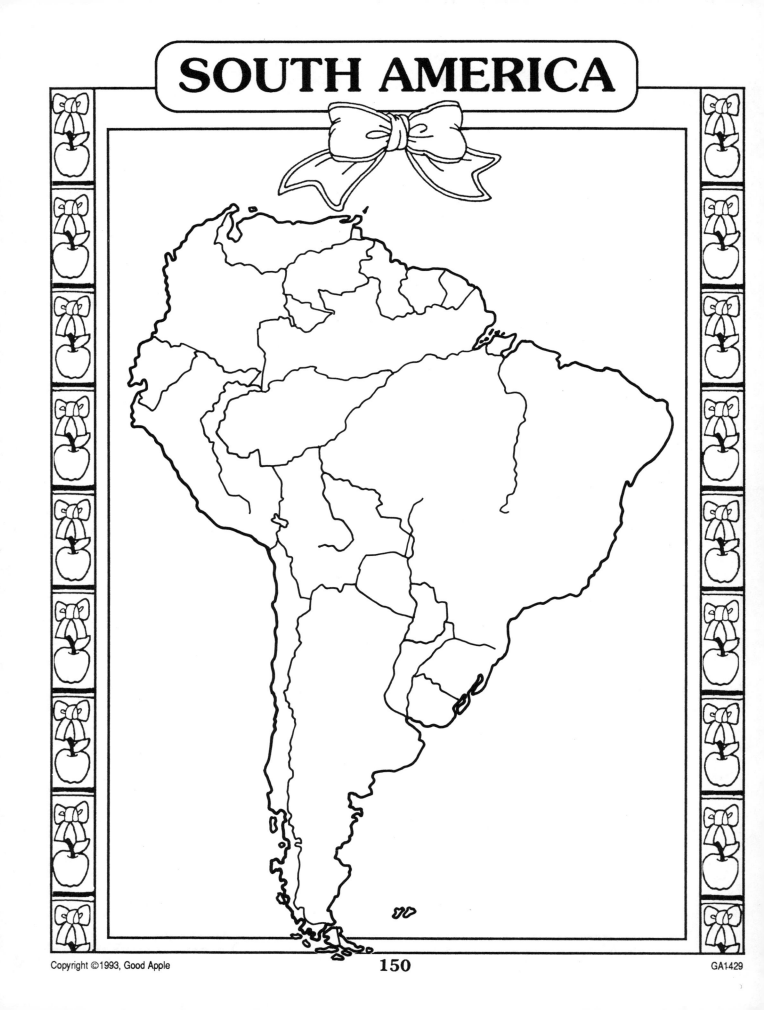

Throughout most Latin American countries, Navidad (Christmas) and Dia de los Tres Reyes (Three Kings' Day) are celebrated with similar traditions and customs. Each country has its own unique traditions influenced by Indians who inhabited each region, but they all share Latin traditions centered around Roman Catholic religious customs.

Bolivia

Christmas celebrations begin on December 1 in Bolivia. Nativity scenes are displayed with *pastoras*, flowers which are similar to poinsettias, surrounding the scenes. Midnight religious services and gifts quietly placed around sleeping children are events that take place on Christmas Eve, December 24.

Brazil

There are no Christmas trees here but Papa Noël, a jolly fellow similar to Santa Claus, though not a primary holiday character associated with the season, visits homes in Brazil.

Many legends have been passed down through generations about this winter holiday. An old Brazilian legend says that on Christmas night animals are endowed with the power of speech, and at the stroke of midnight a rooster crows, "Christo nasceu" meaning "Christ is born." A bull asks, "Onde?" (Where?), and sheep answer, "En Belem de Juda" (In Bethlehem of Judea).

Ecuador

In Ecuador, Christmas and New Year's are celebrated as one. Everyone dresses in holiday attire and gifts are shared with both the rich and the poor. Shoes are placed in windows by hopeful children for gifts left in the night by the passing Christ Child. Firecrackers, noisemakers, bands, and dancing in the streets are traditional customs prior to a midnight religious service and holiday dinner.

Venezuela

On December 16 Venezuelan families bring their *nacimientos* or *pesebres*, Nativity scenes, out of storage and place them in prominent places in their homes. They attend Misas de Aguinaldo, religious Christmas carol services, for nine nights. Exploding firecrackers and ringing bells call worshippers to predawn services and the last service is held on Christmas Eve, Nochebuena de Navidad.

GA1429

Talking Animal Cards

Provide children with the patterns below, scissors, glue, and colored construction paper to make holiday greeting cards.

1. Color and cut out the patterns.
2. Fold a sheet of construction paper in half for each card.
3. Glue an animal and a speech bubble on the front.
4. Write a holiday message in the bubble and sign each card.

GA1429

Provide children with small balloons, paint, glitter, glue, water, and dry beans or rice to make colorful papier-mâché noisemakers.

1. Blow up a small balloon.
2. Layer strips of newspaper dipped in adhesive—one part white glue, one-half part water—over the balloon. Do not cover the knot.
3. Pour a handful of dry beans or rice in the hole.
4. Close the hole with layers of newspapers and allow to dry.
5. Decorate your noisemaker with paint and glitter.

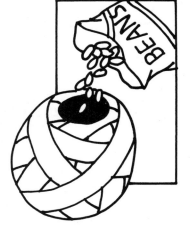

GA1429

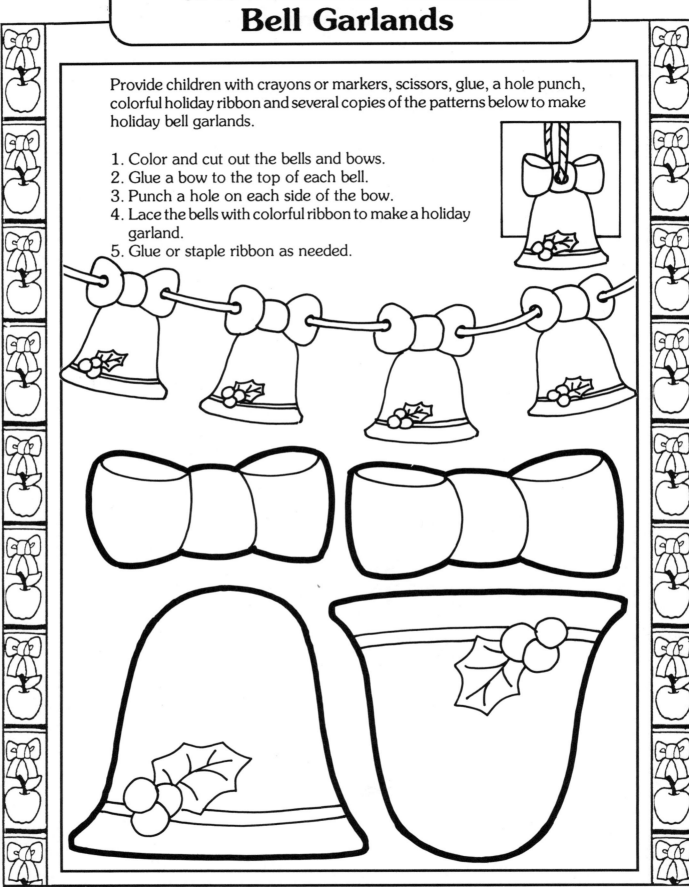

Provide children with crayons or markers, scissors, glue, a hole punch, colorful holiday ribbon and several copies of the patterns below to make holiday bell garlands.

1. Color and cut out the bells and bows.
2. Glue a bow to the top of each bell.
3. Punch a hole on each side of the bow.
4. Lace the bells with colorful ribbon to make a holiday garland.
5. Glue or staple ribbon as needed.

GA1429

Worldwide, Christmas is traditionally a celebration of religious origins. Many cultures display Nativity scenes in homes, shop windows, and religious meeting places.

The center of the scene is the manger where the Christ Child lay. His mother and father, Mary and Joseph, are either standing or kneeling figures as well as shepherds, animals, angels, and the three kings are also included in some displays.

Reproduce the patterns on pages 156-162 for student-made classroom Nativity scenes or as take-home displays.

To make a cardboard box stable:
1. Cover a cardboard box with brown and yellow strips of construction paper.
2. Glue brown strips of construction paper inside the box to make it look like a stable.
3. Glue uneven strips of yellow construction paper to the bottom of the box for straw.

Ask students to bring medium-sized boxes to school to cover with brown or green construction paper strips to resemble straw.

Provide students with crayons or markers, scissors, glue, and oaktag to make the figures sturdy.

1. Color and cut out the patterns.
2. Glue each pattern to a sheet of oaktag and cut around the figure.
3. Cut a slit in each stand where indicated and slide a figure into the slit to make the figure free-standing.
4. Arrange the figure in a cardboard box stable.

GA1429

1. Color and cut out the patterns.
2. Glue each pattern to a sheet of oaktag and cut around the figure.
3. Cut a slit in each stand where indicated and slide a figure into the slit to make the figure free-standing.
4. Arrange the figure in a cardboard box stable.

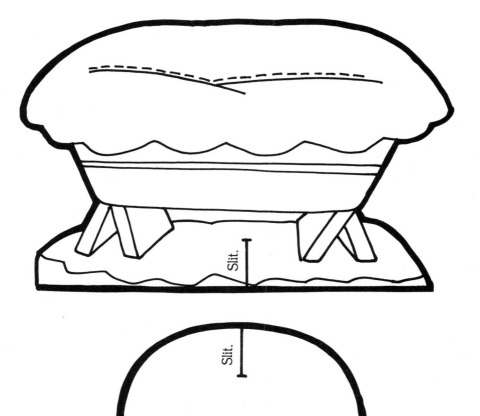

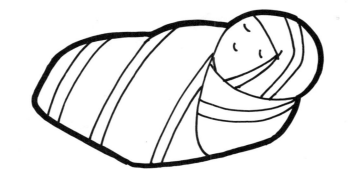

Shepherds

1. Color and cut out the patterns.
2. Glue each pattern to a sheet of oaktag and cut around the figure.
3. Cut a slit in each stand where indicated and slide a figure into the slit to make the figure free-standing.
4. Arrange the figure in a cardboard box stable.

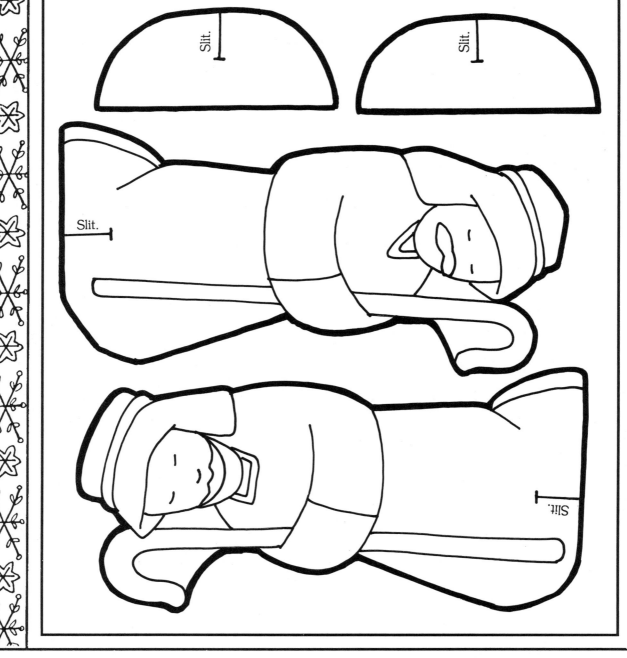

GA1429

Stable Animals

1. Color and cut out the patterns.
2. Glue each pattern to a sheet of oaktag and cut around the figure.
3. Cut a slit in each stand where indicated and slide a figure into the slit to make the figure free-standing.
4. Arrange the figure in a cardboard box stable.

Slit.

Slit.

Slit.

Slit.

GA1429

1. Color and cut out the patterns.
2. Glue each pattern to a sheet of oaktag and cut around the figure.
3. Cut a slit in each stand where indicated and slide a figure into the slit to make the figures free-standing.
4. Arrange the figures in a cardboard box stable.

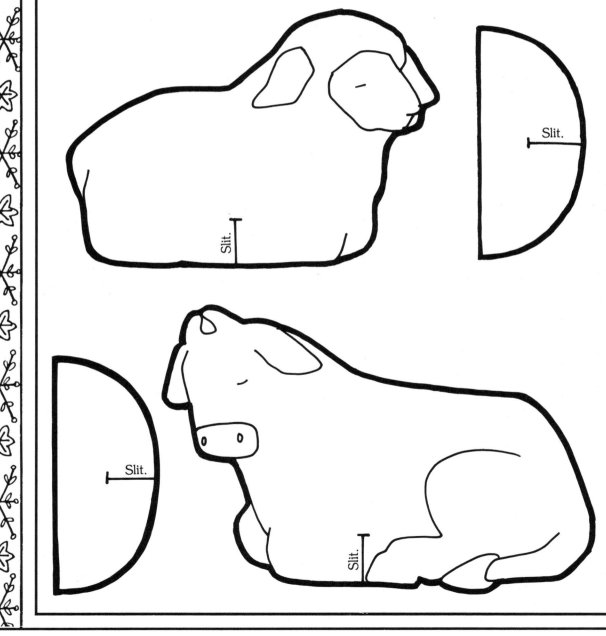

GA1429

1. Color and cut out the patterns.
2. Glue each pattern to a sheet of oaktag and cut around the figure.
3. Cut a slit in each stand where indicated and slide a figure into the slit to make the figure free-standing.
4. Arrange the figure in a cardboard box stable.

Slit.

Fold.

Fold.

Fold.

GA1429

Gaspar, Balthasar, Melchior

1. Color and cut out the patterns.
2. Glue each pattern to a sheet of oaktag and cut around the figure.
3. Cut a slit in the stand where indicated and slide the figure into the slit to make the figure free-standing.
4. Arrange the figure in a cardboard box stable.

Slit.

Slit.

GA1429

CHRISTMAS IN
South America

GLOBAL CHRISTMAS SYMBOLS

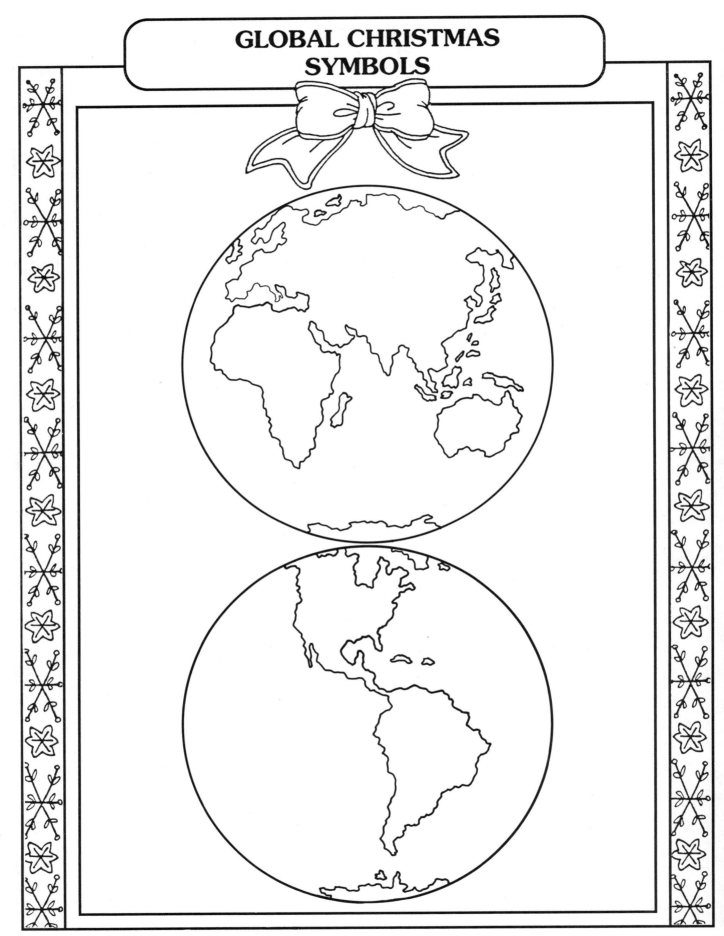

Reproduce the directions on this page for each child and his or her choice patterns from pages 166-181 to create holiday ornaments, displays, and gifts for classroom and take-home projects.

Provide students with a variety of craft supplies to encourage individual creativity.

For classroom displays:
1. Color and cut out the pattern/s.
2. Decorate with glitter, buttons, yarn, and ribbon.
3. Display on windows, doors, or your classroom bulletin board.

For holiday mobiles:
1. Color and cut out the pattern/s.
2. Punch a hole at the top and tie a length of yarn for hanging on a hanger.

For holiday poem covers:
1. Color and cut out the pattern/s.
2. Glue the pattern to the front of a manila file folder.
3. Write the title of your poem at the top.
4. Write your holiday poem on a separate sheet of paper.
5. Glue it to the inside of the folder.

For holiday place mats:
1. Color and cut out the pattern/s.
2. Draw a colorful border around a sheet of 12" x 18" (30.48 x 45.72 cm) construction paper.
3. Arrange and glue the pattern/s on the construction paper.
4. Write a holiday message at the top and laminate for reuse.

GA1429

Angels

1. Color and cut out the patterns.
2. Choose a project and follow the directions for ornaments, greetings, and gifts.

GA1429

GLOBAL CHRISTMAS SYMBOLS
Bells

1. Color and cut out the patterns.
2. Choose a project and follow the directions for ornaments, greetings, and gifts.

GA1429

1. Color and cut out the patterns.
2. Choose a project and follow the directions for ornaments, greetings, and gifts.

1. Color and cut out the patterns.
2. Choose a project and follow the directions for ornaments, greetings, and gifts.

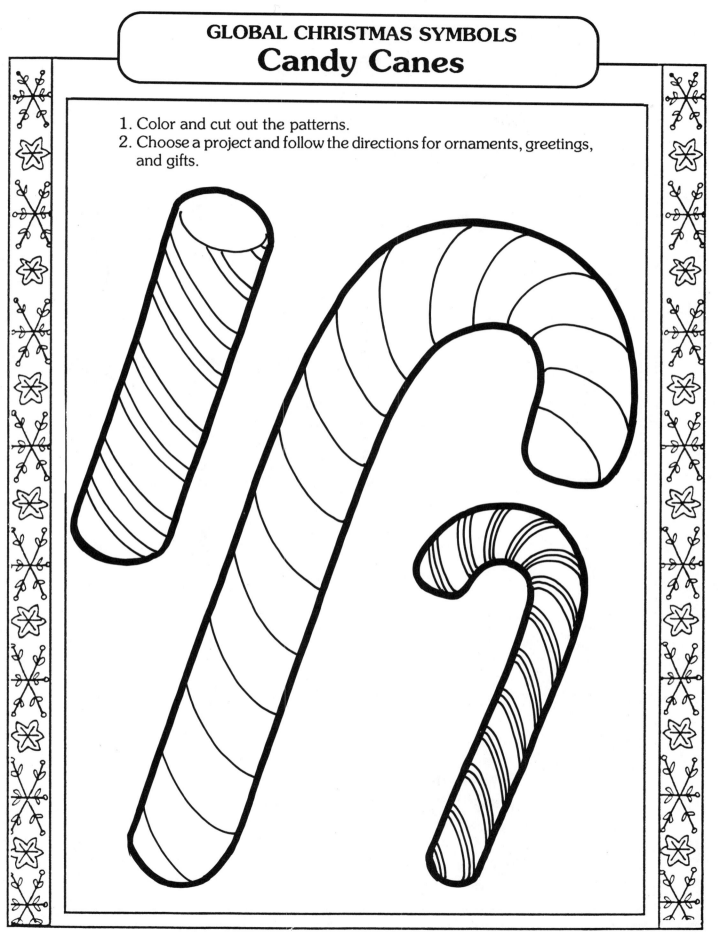

GA1429

1. Color and cut out the patterns.
2. Choose a project and follow the directions for ornaments, greetings, and gifts.

170

1. Color and cut out the patterns.
2. Choose a project and follow the directions for ornaments, greetings, and gifts.

GA1429

1. Color and cut out the patterns.
2. Choose a project and follow the directions for ornaments, greetings, and gifts.

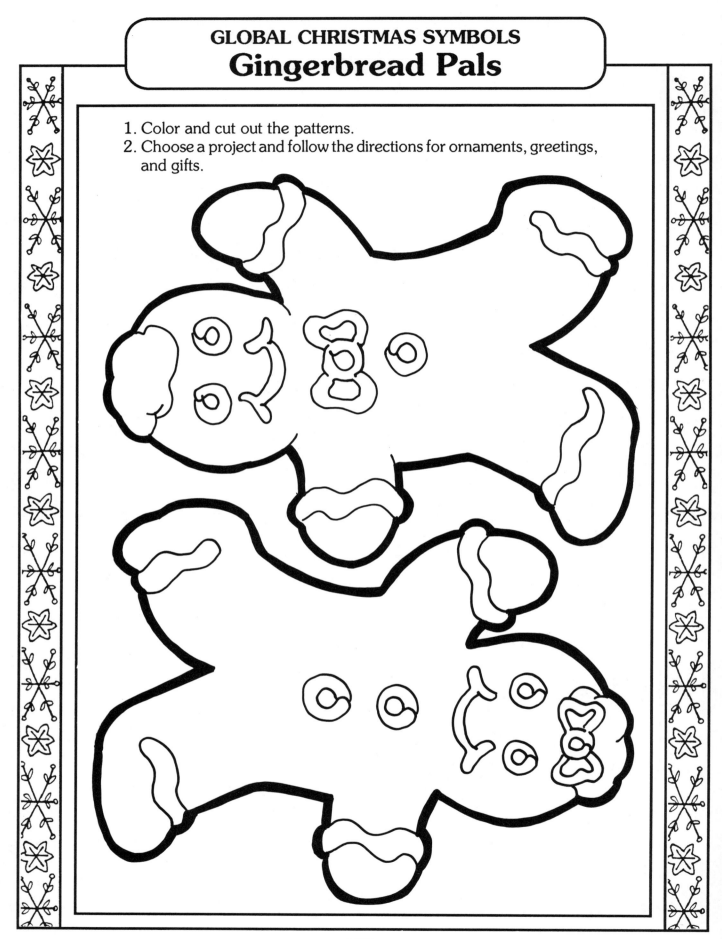

1. Color and cut out the pattern.
2. Choose a project and follow the directions for ornaments, greetings, and gifts.

GA1429

Ornaments

1. Color and cut out the patterns.
2. Choose a project and follow the directions for ornaments, greetings, and gifts.

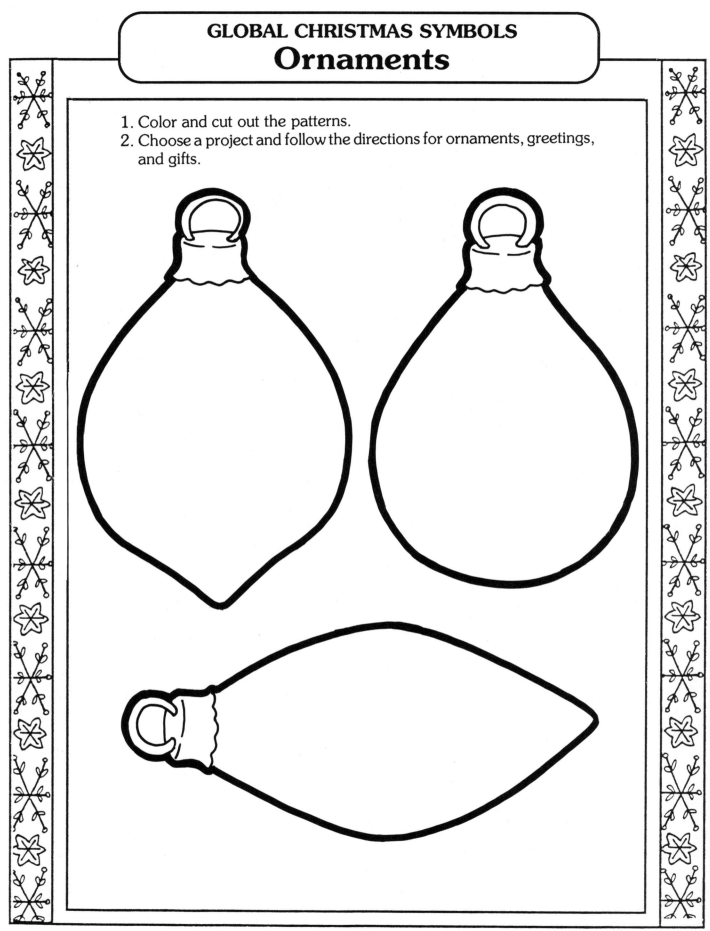

GA1429

1. Color and cut out the patterns.
2. Choose a project and follow the directions for ornaments, greetings, and gifts.

GA1429

1. Color and cut out the pattern.
2. Choose a project and follow the directions for ornaments, greetings, and gifts.

GA1429

1. Color and cut out the pattern.
2. Choose a project and follow the directions for ornaments, greetings, and gifts.

GA1429

1. Color and cut out the pattern.
2. Choose a project and follow the directions for ornaments, greetings, and gifts.

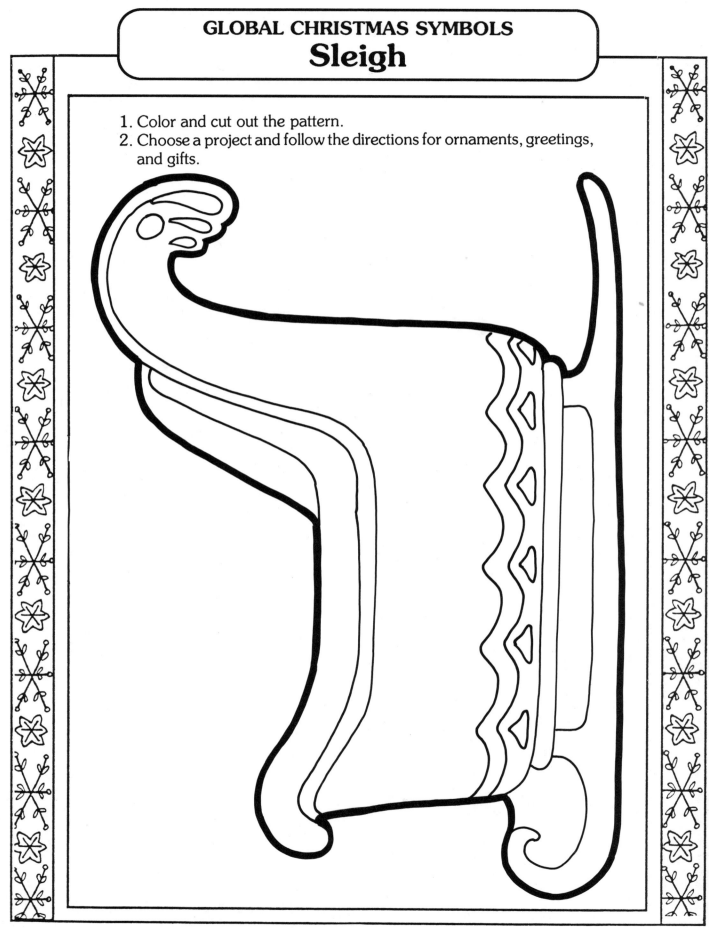

GA1429

1. Color and cut out the pattern.
2. Choose a project and follow the directions for ornaments, greetings, and gifts.

GA1429

Stocking

1. Color and cut out the pattern.
2. Choose a project and follow the directions for ornaments, greetings, and gifts.

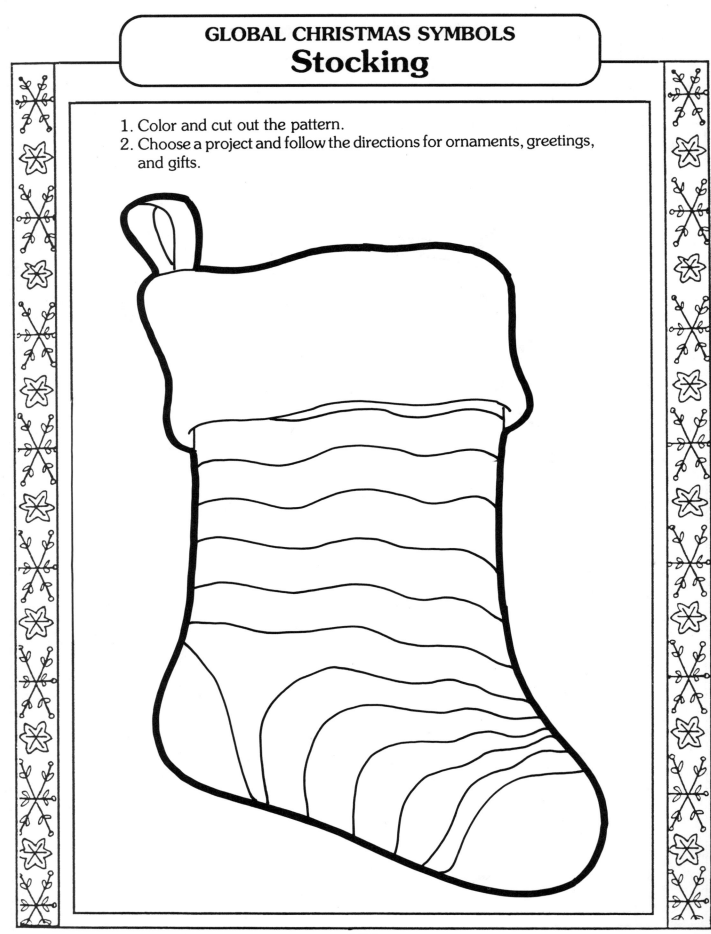

GA1429

1. Color and cut out the pattern.
2. Choose a project and follow the directions for ornaments, greetings, and gifts.

GA1429

GLOBAL CHRISTMAS SYMBOLS
The Twelve Days of Christmas

Create a unique bulletin board display or have children make greeting cards and ornaments with The Twelve Days of Christmas patterns on pages 183-186. Have children work in groups to color, cut out, and glue the patterns to construction paper shapes and pin or staple to the bulletin board in a tree shape as shown below.

Provide students with patterns, crayons or markers, construction paper, glue, a hole punch, and yarn or ribbon to make the displays, cards or ornaments.

GA1429

GLOBAL CHRISTMAS SYMBOLS
The Twelve Days of Christmas

For an ornament:
1. Color and cut out the patterns.
2. Glue each pattern to a colored construction paper shape.
3. Punch a hole at the top of each pattern and tie a length of yarn for a hanging tree ornament.

For a greeting card:
1. Color and cut out the patterns.
2. Glue a pattern to the front of a folded and decorated sheet of construction paper.
3. Write a holiday greeting on the front and a message inside.

GA1429

For an ornament:
1. Color and cut out the patterns.
2. Glue each pattern to a colored construction paper shape.
3. Punch a hole at the top of each pattern and tie a length of yarn for a hanging tree ornament.

For a greeting card:
1. Color and cut out the patterns.
2. Glue a pattern to the front of a folded and decorated sheet of construction paper.
3. Write a holiday greeting on the front and a message inside.

GA1429

For an ornament:
1. Color and cut out the patterns.
2. Glue each pattern to a colored construction paper shape.
3. Punch a hole at the top of each pattern and tie a length of yarn for a hanging tree ornament.

For a greeting card:
1. Color and cut out the patterns.
2. Glue a pattern to the front of a folded and decorated sheet of construction paper.
3. Write a holiday greeting on the front and a message inside.

GA1429

For an ornament:
1. Color and cut out the patterns.
2. Glue each pattern to a colored construction paper shape.
3. Punch a hole at the top of each pattern and tie a length of yarn for a hanging tree ornament.

For a greeting card:
1. Color and cut out the patterns.
2. Glue a pattern to the front of a folded and decorated sheet of construction paper.
3. Write a holiday greeting on the front and a message inside.

GA1429